FUNDAMENTALS OF COUNSELING

DANTES/DSST* Test Study Guide

All rights reserved. This Study Guide, Book and Flashcards are protected under the US Copyright Law. No part of this book or study guide or flashcards may be reproduced, distributed or stored in a retrieval system, or transmitted in any form or by any means, electronic, mechanical, photocopying, recording, or otherwise, without the prior written permission of the publisher Breely Crush Publishing, LLC.

© 2026 Breely Crush Publishing, LLC

DSST is a registered trademark of The Thomson Corporation and its affiliated companies, and does not endorse this book.

971010620143

Copyright ©2003 - 2026, Breely Crush Publishing, LLC.

All rights reserved.

This Study Guide, Book and Flashcards are protected under the US Copyright Law. No part of this publication may be reproduced, distributed or stored in a retrieval system, or transmitted in any form or by any means, electronic, mechanical, photocopying, recording, or otherwise, without the prior written permission of the publisher Breely Crush Publishing, LLC.

Published by Breely Crush Publishing, LLC
10808 River Front Parkway
South Jordan, UT 84095
www.breelycrushpublishing.com

ISBN-10: 1-61433-666-0
ISBN-13: 978-1-61433-666-2

Printed and bound in the United States of America.

DSST is a registered trademark of The Thomson Corporation and its affiliated companies, and does not endorse this book.

Table of Contents

History of Counseling 1
Counseling Psychology 3
Clinical Psychology 4
Structuralism 5
Branches of Counseling 6
Counseling as a Profession 11
Alcoholics Anonymous 11
ACA 13
CACREP 14
NBCC 15
APA 16
ASCA 17
Consultations 18
Group Counseling 22
Family Therapy 24
Virginia Satir 25
Murray Bowen 27
Triangulation 29
Advocacy 30
Counseling Relationship 32
Trust 32
Verbal and Nonverbal Behavior 33
Personality and Characteristics of Counselors 33
Communication 37
The Counseling Environment 40
Empathy 41
Authenticity 43
Confidentiality 43
Transference & Countertransference 44
Ethics and Legal Issues 46
Tarasoff v. University of California 48
Culture in Counseling 49
Different Approaches in Therapy 58
Psychoanalytic Theory 59
Alfred Adler 60
Carl Jung 61
Humanistic Therapy 62
Existential Therapy 63
Logotherapy 65
Gestalt Therapy 67
Phenemenological Approach 70
Cognitive Behavioral Therapy 70

Rational Emotive Behavior Therapy *73*
Systems Therapy *77*
Eclectic Theory *78*
Holistic Therapy *79*
Spiritual Health *81*
Feminist Therapy *81*
Religion in Therapy *84*
Discrimination *86*
AIDS *89*
Substance Abuse *90*
Abuse *93*
Career Development *93*
Trait and Factor Theory *95*
Decision Making *95*
Albert Bandura *96*
Sociological Approach *97*
Personality Approach *97*
Ann Roe *98*
John Holland *99*
Developmental Approaches *100*
Donald Super *101*
Career Education *102*
Human Development *103*
Instinct Theory *105*
Jean Piaget *105*
Piaget's Relevant Definitions *106*
Piaget's Stages of Development *108*
Maslow's Hierarchy of Needs *110*
Freud's Psychosexual Stages *111*
Karen Horney *112*
Kohlberg's Theory of Moral Development *114*
Carol Gilligan *115*
Social Learning Theory *116*
Counseling Today *116*
Assessment & Appraisal Techniques *117*
Observation *122*
History of Assessments *124*
DSM-IV *126*
Sample Test Questions *128*
Test-Taking Strategies *192*
Test Preparation *193*
Legal Note *194*
References *194*

History of Counseling

The development of counseling and psychology as a field of study can be traced as it evolved in three main branches: vocational counseling, counseling psychology and clinical psychology. In many cases, the developments in different areas of psychology were concurrent or overlapping, making it difficult to keep them entirely distinct. Although today the fields do tend to have a fair amount of overlap and integration, it becomes easier to trace their development when considered separately. It is important to understand, however, that in practice the three branches are rarely considered as distinctly as they will be here.

Clinical psychology describes the treatment of mentally ill individuals. It also extends to the study of other behavioral anomalies and psychiatric problems. For example, clinical psychology includes the treatment of problems such as schizophrenia and depression. Because clinical psychology has such a strong focus on mental processes, it tends to be more scientific and laboratory-based. However, clinical psychologists can also help individuals with more minor problems and are trained in psychotherapy and other psychological approaches to allow them to be of the most possible help to their patients.

Although the term counseling psychology can be used to broadly refer to all fields relating to the counseling profession, in this case, it is used to describe treatments involving the psychological health of an individual. Typically, the greatest distinction between clinical and counseling psychology is that the work of a counseling psychologist has its emphasis in treating otherwise healthy individuals who are struggling with problems of a psychological nature. For example, counseling psychology deals with issues which relate to anxiety, grieving, divorce, anger management, cultural issues, or any other factor which relates to the psychological and social development and health of an individual (again though, there are many people who use the two terms interchangeably).

Counseling psychology essentially evolved directly out of the field of vocational counseling. Vocational counseling, which can also be referred to as career counseling, has its focus in helping individuals choose the most productive and satisfying career paths for themselves. Because of this it tends to have a large focus on education of the patient both in the academic sense, and about psychological matters (for this reason, much of counseling psychology is also education related, and focuses on how the mind learns habits and interprets situations).

The origins of vocational counseling can be traced back to the work of **Frank Parsons**. Frank Parsons has often been referred to as the father of counseling. Parsons lived during the early part of the twentieth century, when many people ended up working low skill factory jobs in cities. He noted that most workers were not satisfied or happy with their work, and he argued that by considering what their interests were, the workers could become more satisfied with their work.

Parsons argued that seeking a vocation rather than hunting for a job would be more beneficial to both the individual workers and to the economy as a whole in the long run. He placed a very strong emphasis on connecting education with work, and the development of practical skills. He encouraged workers to first consider what their skills were, and what type of work would make them happy. He also believed that workers should then keep themselves up to date about the job opportunities available to them.

Around this same time is when movements began to make public education compulsory, and as more children began attending school, guidance counselors became a more important part of education. Education began to be viewed as an avenue through which children were prepared for their future jobs, and through which they had the opportunity to become more successful and productive members of society. Due to Parson's work during this time, counseling became a true profession, with its roots in vocational guidance and training. The same principles which Parsons advocated are still the basis of vocational therapy today.

Another individual whose work was important in bringing counseling into schools was Jesse B. Davis. Davis became the principal of a high school and strongly encouraged teachers to give their students aptitude tests. Davis also encouraged them to give students assignments and encourage a growing interest in different career paths. He is considered to be the first person to implement systematic vocational counseling in a school.

The next major step in vocational counseling was made by Ann Roe. Although Roe had little actual interest in the field of career choice, much of her theory revolved around the concept of job satisfaction. Roe's work was heavily influenced by psychoanalytic theory, and focused on the relationship that a parent has with their child. According to Roe, people choose their eventual careers to fulfill a psychological need which developed as a result of this parent-child relationship (along with, to a certain extent, genetics, education, and other factors).

The presence of counselors in schools evolved from a number of events throughout the 1960s until the 1980s. Integrating first into elementary schools, and then later into middle schools and high schools. With time, the role of these counselors expanded to include specialized vocational guidance, general counseling and the treatment of mental health issues.

Although vocational therapy is available to all individuals, it is particularly available to adolescents through school vocational counselors. This is the case for a number of reasons. It was once believed that vocational decisions were made at a single point in a person's life; however, now the understanding is that career decisions are a result of choices and experiences that a person has throughout their childhood.

Educators and counselors should be continuously encouraging and aiding adolescents in their approach to careers. Helping individuals choose fulfilling careers both improves their future happiness, and the productivity of the economy. It is also especially important that vocational counseling be available in schools because decisions that are made during education, such as which classes to take and which goals to pursue, have a significant impact on the opportunities available to them in the future.

In order to be of most help to students, there are a number of tasks which vocational counselors must consider. For example, they should keep updated about the job market so they can effectively counsel a student. They should also keep accurate records of the students' progress, and keep in touch with parents and teachers about any concerns related to the student. It is vital that the counselor instill a sense of the importance of education and prepare them for future experiences.

 Counseling Psychology

Freud established a practice for studying and treating patients with psychological difficulties in the 1880s. Although many of his methods and theories have remained highly controversial over the years, no other individual has had such a profound impact on the field of psychology. His psychoanalytic theory became the starting point or basis for many theories which have since developed.

After Freud, many different individuals began developing theories, some of the most important of which include Carl Rogers (who developed the person-centered theory) and Carl Jung. Ironically, both of these individuals studied under Freud, but were disowned by him when they chose to branch off with their own philosophies.

Although these theories were developed and used over the next half-century, what really allowed the counseling psychology profession to take off were the events of World War II. During the war, the military needed an effective method for placing soldiers. Intelligence and other types of standardized tests began to evolve (initially for the use of vocational counselors) which were used for this purpose. This created a branching of vocational counseling to counseling psychology.

In addition, the events after WWII had an impact on counseling psychology. Many of the soldiers returning from the war suffered two difficulties. Firstly, they needed vocational guidance and training to reintegrate into normal life. Secondly, many suffered from severe psychological distress following the war.

The federal government decided to jointly solve these problems by instituting a division of counseling psychology to work with individuals. The division provided both training and employment for counseling psychologists. It is for these that the field of counseling psychology is considered to have evolved from vocational counseling. The focus of counseling psychology became to help individuals in their daily life struggles, and to teach them both how to be productive members of society, and how to overcome their psychological struggles.

Clinical Psychology

Dorothea Dix, who devoted her life to improving the treatment of mentally ill individuals, made large strides in the development of clinical psychology. Dix originally worked in the field of education. In the mid-1800s, she volunteered to teach Sunday school classes for women in a local prison. It was here that she witnessed the appalling treatment of mentally ill individuals.

At the time, there was little understanding of the causes of mental illness, and even less was understood about its treatment. For example, it was commonly believed that it was entirely untreatable and that mentally ill individuals did not feel pain or cold. As a result, the mentally ill (or, at the very least, those not from wealthy families) were kept in cold, dark cells with little food and in close proximity to all other types of criminals. Often they were whipped or subjected to other forms of disciplinary measures to illicit their compliance. Dix spent the rest of her life working to improve the treatment of mentally ill individuals.

She did this by demonstrating that placing them in caring environments (where they could be watched over and taken care of) would often reduce or eliminate symptoms. Although there was still no scientific understanding of the effects of various mental illnesses, and there would still be a long road ahead before the mentally ill were given truly humane treatment, this was a large step towards increasing interest and improving treatments and attitudes towards it. Due to her work more than 30 hospitals for mentally ill patients were built.

Another important step in the history of treating mental illness was the work of **Wilhelm Wundt** in the late 1870s. Wundt established the first laboratory for studying the mind, which made it a much more reputable and concrete field. For this he is known as the father of experimental psychology. Wundt's main contribution to the field of psychology was the theory of structuralism.

Structuralism

Structuralism was essentially the first major school of thought in psychology, but it was soon followed by many additional theories (in fact, within ten years of Wundt establishing his laboratory, Freud had begun his practice as well). Wundt was aided in his work by Edward B. Titchener. The goal of structuralism is to break down the functions of the mind into their most basic components (like scientists break molecules into atoms).

The main criticism of Wundt's work, and the reason for which it quickly faded, was its methods. Wundt and Titchener's studies of structuralism relied primarily on introspection, which was considered an unreliable and ineffective method. Their research essentially consisted of individuals examining their thought processes and responses (introspection) and trying to deconstruct their reactions to the basic impulse behind them.

Between the influences of Dix, Wundt, and others, mental institutions for the care of mentally ill individuals became much more common. However, there was still little understanding of its causes, and little knowledge of how to treat it. Although many institutions began with high ideals of treatment, many were subject to overcrowding and less humane methods were often reinstated.

This pattern of inadequate and inhumane treatment climaxed leading to the deinstitutionalization movement of the 20th century. The deinstitutionalization movement refers to a shift in philosophy from putting patients in state-run, long-term care facilities, to placing them in more localized community facilities offering outpatient care.

There are a number of reasons for the shift. One important factor is the bad reputation that state institutions had developed. These facilities were almost always overcrowded, understaffed, and underfunded. Funding was especially cut during times of war, and patients received seriously inadequate care, with many even starving to death. As awareness about these issues became more widespread, the natural tendency was concern.

A second, possibly more important, factor spurring the deinstitutionalization movement was the origination of psychiatric medicine in the 1950s which was able to reduce the chronic symptoms of many disorders, which made long term care unnecessary for many patients. Because the medications could mask the symptoms, patients were able to function adequately in regular society.

As the study of intelligence and the brain became more possible and popular following WWII, the treatment of mental illnesses began to integrate with other forms of psychology. Also, people tended to be fairly protective of those returning from war with psychological problems, and their treatment was more monitored. Scientific developments spurred the belief that mental illnesses were treatable and curable, and this caused them to be increasingly integrated with the study of other areas of psychology.

Branches of Counseling

To state it most simply, counseling is all about advice. While other branches of psychology such as therapy and psychiatry are similarly concerned with understanding the importance and effect of mental processes and the behavior of individuals, counseling has the specific intent and focus of advising clients and helping them to attain their full potential. Counselors work with clients to help them become able to handle their problems independently, whether by increasing conflict resolution skills, identifying recurring negative behaviors, or any other number of problems. As a result, counseling as a profession tends to have a somewhat wider focus than any other area of psychology.

The classification of therapist, for example, is generally applied to situations in which some form of treatment is being applied. Consider that there are distinctions of music therapy, physical therapy, yoga therapy, psychoanalytical therapy, reality therapy, group therapy, and an essentially endless list of additional classifications. In each case, the goal is to treat individuals using some predefined method. Contrast this with a psychiatrist who focuses specifically on the physical causes of mental illnesses, and studies different ways of addressing the problem from a medical perspective. The classification of psychiatrist is therefore characterized by a focus on pathology. That is, the diagnosis of a problem.

Counseling, then, is essentially a hybrid of these two areas of study. Counselors will consider both pathological factors and situational factors as they affect a client's overall mental, physical and social health. This creates a great diversity in the problems which counselors will face in their practice. They may be required to work with either mentally ill individuals or otherwise healthy individuals who are simply struggling to cope with a situation which has arisen in their life. The matters which they give counsel about may range from vocational matters, to interpersonal skills, to substance abuse, to stress and anxiety, and so on.

In terms of preparation to become a counselor (i.e., education and licensure issues) the requirements are set at a state level and can vary widely. However, in almost all cases a minimum of a master's degree in counseling is required to become a licensed counselor. Of course, the more education and experience a person has, the more professional opportunities are available to them (and at a better pay).

Based on the specific field in which a person wishes to focus, that degree can be in a number of counseling fields. These include degrees specific to school counseling (either secondary or elementary), marriage and family counseling, career counseling, mental health counseling, and many other fields as well. Most counseling degrees require that an individual gains clinical experience in addition to their academic studies.

For a person interested in a profession related to counseling, there are a number of relevant degrees which they may seek. For example, psychologists must complete a path of study that is highly similar to counselors, but is more in depth. In order to become a psychologist, a person must also complete a master's degree in a counseling or psychology related field, and undergo several years of clinical experience.

Moving beyond the basic master's degree, psychologists must also complete a Ph.D. The two degrees that are most typically thought of in relation to psychology are a Ph.D. in psychology or a Psy.D. Both degrees are doctorates which a person can earn, but with slightly different emphasis (the Ph.D. has more of an emphasis in research, whereas the Psy.D. has more of an emphasis in practice). However, both are valid for a person seeking to become a counselor or psychologist, and they open up a wide degree of options in career choices.

In addition to basic education, most states also require some form of licensing or certification in order for a person to be a practicing counselor. Licensure requirements are determined by the state and field in which a counselor practices. The most commonly encouraged form of licensing is an NCC, or National Certified Counselor license. It is awarded by the National Board for Certified Counselors (NBCC) to individuals who have a graduate degree, two years of experience, and have passed an exam. The NBCC requires that counselors either retake the exam or complete a certain amount of additional education in order to maintain certification.

Although the development of counseling as a profession spans centuries, the development was not complete until licensure requirements came into effect. In 1943, the APA established a division dedicated to the field of counseling which officially set it apart from other branches of psychology.

The APA's Division of Counseling and Guidance was a great step towards establishing counseling as a distinct profession, but licensure was still not a requirement. Such requirements began in 1945 with the state of Connecticut which required that counselors and psychologists be professionally licensed. Shortly following these licensure requirements in Connecticut, the state of California began to require the registration of counselors and psychologists with the state. Many other states followed with time, allowing counseling to develop into the field that it is today.

As the discussion of education and qualifications suggests, there is a great variety in the types of counseling available. Based on the area of specialty, a counselor will be faced with different expectations, and be required to fulfill different roles. Part of the reason that the field of counseling as a whole is so varied is just this. As society changes and evolves, as it does continually, the needs of its members change. New challenges, stresses, goals, values, and problems are continually emerging which result in the development of new branches and emphases in counseling. For example, some of the different branches which counselors can be classified into include school counselors, vocational counselors, rehabilitation counselors, marriage and family counselors, and mental health counselors.

The type of counselor which most individuals are familiar with is a school counselor. School counselors are the most common types of counselors in the United States. A school counselor will work with students in both preparing for future educational roles, future career paths, and dealing with the stresses and challenges of the educational process. Based on the level at which the counselor works they may help students in exploring their interests, provide them with information about colleges, and teach career planning, resume, and writing skills.

The educational or informative role of school counselors is an important one; however, also expected of school counselors is competence in handling social concerns that affect students. The role of school counselors extends to the role of confidant in some cases, and they may work with students who are suffering from depression, interpersonal problems, anxiety, or severe health concerns. It is also important that counselors are tuned into issues involving abusive situations. Counselors can be instrumental in identifying situations in which abuse may be occurring.

As societal problems such as drug abuse, sexual identity, eating disorders, and others become more common among students, school counselors must become increasingly competent in effectively handling these matters. This includes becoming familiar with the associated techniques, practices, and ethical issues, as well as being empathetic and able to identify with students.

Another form of counselor is a vocational counselor. Vocational counselors are also referred to as career counselors. The field of career counseling has the specific focus of helping individuals with their career options. A person would typically go to a career counselor if they are considering changing jobs, having difficulties holding jobs, having difficulties finding a job that suits them, or simply planning for the future. A career counselor will get to know their client and understand their personality, interests, skills and situation. They may use devices such as an aptitude test to help them learn more quickly and succinctly about the individual client.

A career counselor needs to have an understanding of the many types of jobs and their qualifications. They will also be expected to be competent in working with clients and encouraging them in their search for a better suited career. The primary role of a career counselor is to aid the client in exploring as many different career paths as possible. This way they can becoming more attuned to what it is that they are looking for, or which will make them happiest.

In order to do this most successfully, an effective career counselor will be able to help clients access a network of employment agencies, training schools, and job preparation services, which can supplement the help that the counselor themselves give. Career counselors will often hold classes to help their clients prepare for work, such as resume preparation, interview skills, job search skills, technical skills (i.e., computer and technology skills), and others. If a counselor determines that a client is likely in need of formal counseling before seeking a job, they should be able to either provide counseling or refer the client to a counselor.

A third group of counselors to consider is rehabilitation counselors. Rehabilitation counselors specialize in working with individuals who either are disabled or are recovering from serious injury. The role of this form of counselor is in helping the individual (such as by providing information and aid) with vocational, educational, and social needs with specific relevance to their situations. Rehabilitation counselors must also fill a role of assessing the client's mental state. They may need to help clients work through feelings of frustration, depression, or anger about their condition as the situation demands. A rehabilitation counselor may be required to coordinate with physicians, nurses, and employers.

A unique set of roles to fulfill also exists for marriage and family counselors. Marriage and family counselors specifically address matters of interpersonal relationships. Some of the roles which they may be required to fulfill include mediator, peacemaker, advisor, and educator. Logically, a large part of the role which marriage and family counselors fill involves conflict resolution. Marriage and family counselors work with couples, individuals, families, and other close-knit groups.

This branch of counseling tends to be highly unique from other branches because rather than focusing on the internal emotional state of a client, marriage and family counselors look at the dynamic of interactions between individuals. While other forms of counseling may consider interpersonal aspects, or engage those with whom the client shares a close relationship in the counseling process, marriage and family therapy has the specific focus of doing so. Marriage and family therapists must have a solid understanding of communication skills, and understand the role of perception and interaction among the members of a group.

Some counselors will also specialize in the treatment of individuals with drug abuse problems. Such counselors are referred to as substance abuse counselors (or occasionally as behavioral disorder counselors). Substance abuse counselors may fulfill many roles in relation to their clients. They may run drug tests in order to monitor their client's activities, and should provide a support system from which the client can begin their recovery. For example, by being open, understanding, and approachable counselors can provide a place for clients to turn when they become discouraged or frustrated.

Substance abuse counselors may also fill an educational role for their clients. Their responsibilities may include educating clients both about the risks and issues associated with drug use and about the resources available to them. For example, they may direct them towards Alcoholics Anonymous meetings, Narcotics Anonymous meetings, or other support groups that exist in the area. This requires that counselors be aware of the opportunities that exist in the areas in which they work. A practice of being attentive and supportive throughout the process, and ensuring that clients have an adequate support system, is an important way that counselors can maintain their clients' success.

An additional branch of counselors, and the type of counselor that people most stereotypically think of, is mental health counselors. Counselors falling under this distinction are most directly involved in treating individuals experiencing emotional conflicts and strains. For example, mental health counselors may address anxiety, depression, grief, post-traumatic stress disorders, trauma, suicidal tendencies, or abuse. Due to the variety of problems which mental health counselors address, mental health counseling is expected to be one of the fastest growing branches of counseling in the future.

Although mental health counselors often work closely with psychiatrists, social workers, and psychologists, they are often considered distinct from other fields because the primary focus of mental health counselors is the prevention of future problems. Mental health counselors work to identify and then minimize the difficulties that clients are struggling with. This can involve techniques ranging from psychoanalytic techniques which identify and correct destructive thought patterns, to simply working with clients to teach them better coping or communication skills.

Because emotional distress is generally a reaction to some outwardly occurring event, mental health counselors will often be called on to address many of the issues which other forms of counselors address. For example, a counselor may determine that their client is feeling depressed as a result of their inability to find an adequate job to support their family. In this case, the counselor may end up taking on the role of vocational counselor in order to best help them (or referring them to a vocational counselor). As another example, a counselor may determine that a client's self-esteem issues stem from an unhealthy relationship with their spouse, in which case they may then seek to incorporate elements of marriage and family counseling into their sessions. These are just two examples of the fact that the factors which lead to mental and emotional strains are often varied and complex, resulting in a fair amount of overlap among the many different fields of counseling.

In addition to different roles and expectations that are associated with different forms of counseling, the work environment of a counselor will also vary with their specific field of interest. School counselors, for example, will spend the majority of their time in schools working with students (either elementary, secondary, or beyond as the case may be). This is quite different from, say, mental health counselors or marriage and family counselors. Counselors in these fields would be much more likely to work in a professional office.

Counseling as a Profession

Any of the different types of counselors may also gain employment in community settings, in which case they may find themselves working in hospitals, at community centers, or in other settings. If a counselor goes on to become a psychologist researching different aspects of human behavior they could find themselves in any number of settings, such as studying the behavior of prison inmates, working with schoolchildren, traveling to different countries, or virtually any other setting that can be imagined.

In terms of the expected salary that a counselor can expect to earn, the average pay varies by the United States Bureau of Labor Statistics reports that the average salary of a counselor in the United States is around 42 thousand dollars. The lower ranges of salaries fall from 25-30 thousand, and the higher ranges can be anywhere from 60-80 thousand and beyond. Counselors who are self-employed, or who are employed by a private practice, will typically have higher salaries than counselors employed by organizations or by the government.

Alcoholics Anonymous

Alcoholics Anonymous (AA) is an organization whose main purpose is to help alcoholics achieve and maintain sobriety. AA began in the early 1930s when Rowland H. visited Swiss psychoanalyst Carl Jung for help with his alcoholism. Jung directed him to the Oxford Group. The Oxford Group was not designed to help alcoholics, but members sought self-improvement by performing self-inventory, admitting fault, making amends, prayer and meditation, and sharing the message with others. Rowland later introduced "Ebby" Edwin T. to the group.

When Ebby was able to successfully stop drinking, he invited a former drinking buddy Bill W. to the group. After Bill stopped drinking, both men began working with alcoholics at Akron City Hospital. Together they formed the beginnings of a gradually growing fellowship that would develop into Alcoholics Anonymous. In 1939, the fellowship published Alcoholics Anonymous, a book written by Bill that explained AA's philosophy and the twelve step theory. Bill emphasized that alcoholism was a malady of mind, emotions and body. This book, along with a number of positive articles and personal success stories, secured the growth of AA.

Currently, AA is an international fellowship with local groups in thousands of communities and members in 150 countries, including men and women of all ages from different social, economic, and cultural backgrounds. There are no dues or fees associated with the membership because AA is self-supported by contributions. Men and women in the AA program share their experiences with alcohol to help each other recover from alcoholism collectively.

Members attend meetings and implement a "twelve step program" to treat their addiction. Today, the twelve step program has been adapted to meet many different forms of addiction, but the original program began with AA in the 1930's. The twelve steps, from admitting you have a problem to a spiritual awakening, are used to treat addictive behavior. The twelve steps as originally published by Alcoholics Anonymous are:

1. We admitted we were powerless over alcohol - that our lives had become unmanageable.

2. Came to believe that a Power greater than ourselves could restore us to sanity.

3. Made a decision to turn our will and our lives over to the care of God as we understood Him.

4. Made a searching and fearless moral inventory of ourselves.

5. Admitted to God, to ourselves, and to another human being the exact nature of our wrongs.

6. Were entirely ready to have God remove all these defects of character.

7. Humbly asked Him to remove our shortcomings.

8. Made a list of all persons we had harmed, and became willing to make amends to them all.

9. Made direct amends to such people wherever possible, except when to do so would injure them or others.

10. Continued to take personal inventory and when we were wrong promptly admitted it.

11. Sought through prayer and meditation to improve our conscious contact with God, as we understood Him, praying only for knowledge of His will for us and the power to carry that out.

12. Having had a spiritual awakening as the result of these Steps, we tried to carry this message to alcoholics, and to practice these principles in all our affairs.

 ACA

Hundreds of professional organizations exist within the fields of psychology and counseling. One of the most important and well-known of these organizations is the American Counseling Association (ACA). The ACA was founded in 1952 under the name American Personnel and Guidance Association, adopting its current name in 1983. Since the time of its founding, the American Counseling Association has become not only the primary representative association for professional counselors within the United States, but also the largest organization representing professional counselors in the world. It is composed of more than 50 thousand members, and 19 chartered divisions and 56 branches (spanning the United States, Latin America, and Europe).

The purpose of the ACA is to help validate and expand the field of counseling. It does this in essentially two different ways. Firstly, by providing an avenue through which research and development can occur in a standardized way. Because of its size, the ACA is widely recognized, which has allowed it to become a stabilizing force in the field of counseling. For example, the ACA is instrumental in determining national ethics and licensing practices. They are often before Congress and other governing bodies to consult on matters related to the counseling profession. They are also affiliated with important corporations to improve the services offered to members. All of these actions allow for increased validity and homogeneity in the field of counseling as a whole.

In addition to the validity which the ACA lends to the counseling profession, it is also instrumental in the growth of counseling, both in terms of the profession and in terms of research and knowledge relating to it. For example, ACA publishes the Journal of

Counseling and Development, which is a widely read and accepted professional journal. The journal includes articles pertaining to the practice of counseling, trends, and theory, in addition to the most recent research in various fields. The Journal of Counseling and Development is just one of the many publications which the ACA publishes or sponsors.

In addition the publications the ACA produces, they also provide training workshops for members. The ACA will often hold national and regional conventions which bring members together and allow the spread of information and ideas. The ACA also includes branches which provide educational opportunities for individuals interested in the counseling profession, and it offers many leadership opportunities.

 CACREP

Another important professional organization is the Council for Accreditation of Counseling and Related Education Programs, more commonly referred to as CACREP. As its name suggested, the primary purpose of CACREP is to accredit counseling programs in the United States. Understanding the role of CACREP requires understanding the two types of accreditation: institutional and specialized. Institutional accreditation is applied to institutions as a whole (a school or university must be accredited in its entirety).

Although CACREP accreditation requires that the program belong to an accredited institution, CACREP is distinct from agencies which offer institutional accreditation. Rather, it is a specialized accreditation agency which specifically evaluates counseling programs. CACREP offers accreditation in seven different graduate level programs. These are Addiction Counseling, Career Counseling, Clinical Mental Health Counseling, Marriage, Couple, Family Counseling, School Counseling, Student Affairs and College Counseling, and Counselor Education and Supervision.

CACREP is currently the only accreditation body endorsed by the ACA, so for many attending a CACREP-accredited program is an important choice. Although the specific standards vary by state, in many cases it is required that an individual complete their degree from a CACREP-accredited program in order to become a licensed counselor. Also, other forms of licensing (such as the NCC) additionally require graduation from an accredited program.

The reason that CACREP accreditation is important for counseling programs is because it ensures that a program is adequately preparing individuals for counseling professions. It is also an assurance to students in the program that the program is both professionally and financially stable. The CACREP focuses on two main standards when evaluating programs: program adequacy and ethical preparations.

In terms of program adequacy, the CACREP is concerned with ensuring that there exists a pattern of excellence in program development, and continuing attempts to improve programs with time. Ensuring that programs are kept up to date is an important element in accreditation. While of course the CACREP does wish to ensure that students are being prepared academically and will graduate with a sufficient knowledge base, the current trend in standards equally emphasizes an experience-based approach.

The CACREP is also concerned with the ethical preparations that are received in counseling programs. To ensure that programs are properly preparing students for a pattern of ethical counseling practice throughout their careers. These considerations are meant to ensure that programs sufficiently teach a need for respect in dealing with patients, and an outlook consistent with ideals of optimal human development. For example, qualities which the CACREP promotes are strong and responsible leadership, fair and consistent decision-making skills, an openness for change and growth, and a respect for society and diversity.

 NBCC

Another important organization to be aware of in the field of counseling is the National Board for the Certification of Counselors and Affiliates, Inc. (NBCC). The primary role of the NBCC is certifying counselors. It was created by the ACA as an independent body in 1982, and has since developed a set of strict standards required for counselors to receive certification. More than 40 thousand counselors across a variety of countries are certified by the NBCC.

Although it is not required in all states, it is highly recommended that all counselors are certified by the NBCC. The primary form of certification which the NBCC offers is referred to as National Counselor Certification (NCC). The NBCC offers a few specialty certifications in addition, but the NCC is the most common. Some of the benefits of NCC certification include that it is a national certification as opposed to state licenses which are only valid at the state level. The NBCC is also involved in a number of advocacy activities which benefit NCC-certified counselors.

NCC certification has three basic requirements. The first requirement is that applicants must complete a master's degree or higher in a counseling related field. The degree must be from an accredited university in order for the NBCC to recognize the degree. The second requirement is closely related to the first. Namely, applicants must have completed at least 48 credits of graduate level classes. The NBCC specifies eight different content areas (e.g., group work, human development, social and cultural foundations, etc.) into which a good portion of these credit hours must fall.

The third requirement is that applicants must have passed the National Counselor Exam (NCE). The NCE is an exam offered by the NBCC. The exam is a four hour, 200 question, multiple choice test. The subject matter on the NCE test falls primarily within the eight content areas that applicants are required to have completed courses in, along with some questions with a more practical base. In addition to being a requirement for NCC certification, the NCE is also used by a number of states as a requirement for state licensing.

Once an individual has completed and passed the NCE, the final requirement to receive NCC certification is the completion (within a three year time frame) of 3,000 hours of work experience, 100 hours of which must be overseen by a qualified supervisor. However, it is important to note that for individuals who attended a CACREP-accredited program, this requirement is waived. (This is one of the important benefits of attending a CACREP-accredited program.)

APA

The American Psychological Association (APA) is another important professional organization within the United States. The APA was founded in 1892 and is a Washington DC-based organization which represents the interests of and works to enhance the applications of the field of psychology. It is represented by 54 different branches which may represent specific categories or interests of psychology divisions (e.g., Division 17 represents counseling psychology).

One of the primary differences between the APA and the ACA is that the ACA works more specifically with making resources available to counselors and ensuring that counselors themselves are practicing ethically and competently. The primary focus of the APA, on the other hand, is in expanding the role and study of psychology within the United States. With this wider ideological base, the APA considers matters regarding psychological research, counseling, and other mental health services. As a result, its goals and procedures are slightly different from the ACA.

The APA's organizational vision includes many different factors. For example, it seeks to serve as a central organization in uniting efforts in the field of psychology, as well as be an inspiring force in spurring new research and study. Along with this study, however, the APA also advocates the use of ethical and dignified practices and techniques in the application of psychology. The APA recognizes three primary goals of its organization. The first goal relates to its effectiveness as an organization. With over 150 thousand members, the APA has a great ability to influence the field of psychology. Structured organization of training programs, monitoring of funds, and proper carrying out of decisions made by the governing board are all essential.

The second goal of the APA relates to expanding and validating the role of psychology in promoting health. Advocating psychology as an important factor in health, working with insurance companies to integrated psychological needs into coverage, and educating both the public and psychologists about the uses and benefits of psychology are all examples of the types of actions taken in regards to this goal. By advocating the importance of psychology, the APA works to bring increasing validity and recognition to counseling and other mental health services as a whole.

The final goal of the APA is in establishing psychology as a scientific endeavor. This goal works hand in hand with the other goals of the APA, as establishing psychology as a scientific pursuit would additionally validate and expand the field. Advocating well-founded research and promoting increasing education and understanding of psychology are important functions of the APA in working towards this goal. As the APA works towards achieving each of these goals they additionally promote values such as a strong ethical culture, pattern of excellence, and attention to diversity all psychology related practices.

 ASCA

Because school counseling is the largest branch of counseling in the United States today, the American School Counselors Association (ASCA) is another important professional organization to be aware of. The ASCA is the branch of the ACA which is specifically concerned with matters involving school counseling. It has over 29,000 members and works to promote good counseling practices among school counselors.

The ASCA serves a number of important functions. One goal of the ASCA is to provide school counselors with access to information and resources that will help them stay up to date and as effective as possible in their practices. They also promote a high level of professionalism, and a strong ethical foundation among counselors. The ASCA works with counselors to enhance skill, conduct research, and advocate in the community.

Many benefits are also available to members of the ASCA. For example, the ASCA publishes a professional journal five times each year which is made available to members. In addition to this journal, the ASCA publishes a monthly magazine which members are given access to, as well as providing discounted prices on numerous other publications and resources. This is in line with the ASCA's goal of keeping counselors up to date on research and information about school counseling. The ASCA also provides members with access to resources that they can use in their practice, such as tape recorders, starter kits, and other materials. Professional development is also encouraged through different training sessions and meetings put on by the ASCA.

Consultations

In addition the matters of education, licensing, and membership in professional organizations, another important role that is a part of the counseling profession is that of consultation. In counseling, consultation can occur in two basic ways. Firstly, consultation can be considered an indirect form of counseling. This is when one counselor is struggling with a client, and consults another counselor for their opinion and advice on how to best help the client. Hence, the consultant (the counselor who is consulted on the issue) is essentially indirectly counseling the client. Their techniques and processes are being passed on to the client through the consultee (the counselor who is directly working with the client).

This form of consultation is most simply described as a collaborative form of counseling. It is important to recognize that within the consultation framework there is no hierarchy that exists (i.e., the consultant is not superior to the consultee, they are working jointly for the mutual benefit of each other and the client). The consultee is under no obligation to act on the advice that they receive from the consultant.

The second framework within which consulting may occur is in counseling of professional individuals. For example, a school teacher is struggling with managing classroom behavior. If she seeks counseling to help her in learning classroom management techniques, or to simply get ideas with how to best handle the students who are causing problems, the counselor is essentially acting as a consultant. Rather than directly seeking to understand and improve the personal life of the client, the counselor is seeking to improve their professional life (and hopefully this will solve any possible existing personal concerns).

In this case as in the first, the consulting relationship is non-hierarchical and has a collaborative nature. Consulting does not technically have to involve a counselor at all; in fact, it occurs within many different professions simply between two professionals within that field. However, it is a common function that counselors fulfill. The primary purpose of consultation is educational. Through consultation, the consultee gains an understanding of how to handle a certain type of situation. This understanding can be carried into future situations and problems. When consulting, counselors should be concerned only with ensuring that a client is advised properly, and that the abilities of the consultee are improved through the experience.

In addition to the professional relationship that exists between consultant and consultee, the relationship of the counselor and client involved in the counseling process similarly takes on a more professional role than in regular therapy. Rather than developing an emotional connection to the client, and seeking to better understand their emotional concerns and reactions, a counselor involved in a consulting role is concerned with the professional aspect of the individual. The relationship has an inherently objective quality.

A number of different models exist to describe the counseling framework. A few of them are the training workshop model, mental health model, process model, and the behavioral model. The first model, the training-workshop model, is essentially just what it sounds like. The training workshop model involves counselors taking time out of their regular work schedules to participate in or organize training retreats. These workshops can take place either at a neutral location away from the office, or within an office with all employees setting aside other work for the duration of the workshop.

While workshops are meant to create a learning environment in which skills and understanding can be improved, they are not meant to be a teaching experience (remember, consultation does not involve a hierarchical relationship between individuals). Rather, training workshops can include practices such as groups of counselors meeting together to discuss questions, concerns, or difficulties that they have encountered. Another possibility would be for groups to observe a counseling process and then discuss different aspects of it in group settings afterward. Training workshops can also be set up for individuals not in the counseling profession, such as teachers, businesspeople, and other professionals.

The second consulting model, the mental health model, is the most commonly used framework in consulting. The mental health model can be broken down into four additional categories of consultation. These are client centered case, consultee centered case, program centered and consultee centered administrative models. Each model is concerned with a different form of relationship within the consulting framework. That is, the different possible structures of relationships between consultants, consultees, and clients.

The client centered case model is used when the services of a consultant are sought in regards to a specific client or case. This model has a specific focus on consulting situations in which a professional counselor (or another professional) comes voluntarily to a consultant seeking advice about a problem (e.g., in the case of a professional counselor they would be asking about a specific client, in the case of teacher they would be asking about problems with a specific students behavior, etc.). The consultant essentially diagnoses the problem for the consultee, and the consultee becomes responsible to then implement their advice and treat the client. The client centered model, then, could be described as a professional seeking a second opinion.

The consultee centered case model is different from the client centered case model because it focuses on difficulties that the consultee is facing as a professional, rather than questions they have about specific clients. In other words, while the consulting emerges as a result of a client situation in which the counselor is struggling, the problem which they are concerned with is a skill or knowledge deficiency of their own, rather than purely a consideration of the client's problem. Here the focus of the consultant is on the consultee, rather than on the client as it would be in the client centered case model.

The third model, the program model, is different from the first two models because it involves more of a dyadic (two person) relationship than a triangular relationship. Also different is the fact that in the first two models, the consultee is typically a counselor or mental health professional, whereas in the program centered model the client is typically a business professional of some sort. The program centered model is a type of expert consultation in which the consultant is needed to help work through organization concerns, such as how to structure a new program or business policy. Because the client is essentially the organization, this consulting model involves the consultant (the expert whose opinion is sought) and the consultee (the businessperson seeking advice). This is the shortest term of the different consulting models.

The final model within the mental health model is the consultee centered administrative model. This model involves a long term effort by a consultant to improve the functioning of an administrative group. Within this model the consultant takes on an active role in identifying organizational problems (be it communication, structure, competency, etc.) and finding ways to alleviate or solve them.

Regardless of the model of consultation used within the mental health framework, the essential purpose of the consultant is to offer an unbiased and objective perspective from which the problem can be solved. The assumption is that those working directly within the situation have become to entrenched and biased to be most efficient at identifying problems and solutions.

Moving beyond the categories of mental health consultation, the next major model of consultation is the process model of consultation. The process model is mainly focused with organizational structures. The consultant in this model is essentially an expert in organizational development. Because it is focused heavily in organizational matters, process consultation heavily emphasizes matters of group interactions. Communication is one of the most important issues addressed by consultants in the process model of consultation. A counselor who is consulting in such situations would seek to help groups of employees, administrators, or others to understand the importance of communication patterns, responsibility, leadership, and interaction patterns.

The final model of consultation which will be discussed is the behavioral model. The behavioral model of consulting pulls heavily from the theories of behavioral counseling theories. For example, one characteristic belief of the behavioral model of consulting is in the inherent relationship between environments and behaviors. The role of the consultant, therefore, is in isolating environmental factors which may be the source of problems in various settings. Because of the environmental focus, this consultation model is most applicable in settings with a regulated or consistent environment (e.g., schools, prisons, hospitals, rehabilitation centers, offices, etc.).

Behavioral consultation also requires identifying a target behavior. Once the behavior that must be changed has been identified, along with the environmental factor encouraging it, the consultant can begin finding ways to modify environments and behavioral beliefs to help consultees in creating the desired results. Along with the assumption that environment has a large impact on behavior is the assumption that all behaviors are learned. Therefore, it is the job of the counselor and consultant to essentially re-educate the client to a more acceptable pattern of behavior.

Because behavioral consultation is so heavily based on analysis of learned behaviors, it tends to follow a systematic and structured approach. The basic framework for how behavioral consultation progresses proceeds involves four different steps: problem identification, problem analysis, plan implementation, and problem evaluation. The first step, problem identification, describes the phase in which the consultee approaches the consultant about the problem that they are working on. They may share information about the case or client, and describe the concerns that they are having.

In the problem analysis phase, the consultant and the consultee will go into more significant depth about the concern. The consultee may need to describe that background of the case, facts about the environment in which the client operates, the problem and target behaviors, details specific to the client that may complicate or enhance counseling, the attempts that have been made and what they involved, and any other useful information that the consultant may need to fully understand the situation. Once the consultant has a more adequate knowledge of the situation, the consultant and consultee can then discuss options, techniques, and theories which could be usefully applied and used in the situation.

After having discussed the case in depth, it is then the responsibility of the consultee to move to the next step – plan implementation. At this point, the consultee would essentially return to the client and continue with the counseling process, simply implementing the plan as discussed with the consultant. In this regard, behavioral consultation becomes closely tied with the theories and techniques of behavioral counseling. For example, some of the techniques which may be applied include reinforcement, shaping, and others.

Reinforcement refers to a pattern of punishment and rewards which are used to encourage or discourage different behaviors. **Positive reinforcement** describes any actions which are intended to increase the occurrence of a behavior and negative reinforcement describes any actions which are intended to decrease the occurrence of a behavior. For example, if the counselor is working with a client to resolve anger management problems, a possible form of negative reinforcement would be to introduce some form of punishment whenever they lose their temper (such as requiring them to write a letter of apology, as a simple example). On the other hand, an example of positive reinforcement could be if, when working with a client suffering from depression, the plan implemented involves some sort of reward for each time they think a positive thought. Reinforcement can be varied across a number of combinations of time schedules, punishments, rewards, and other factors.

The **shaping** technique involves generating a gradual change in behavior patterns. Shaping can also be referred to as successive approximation. Essentially how shaping works is by reinforcing gradual changes towards a desired behavior. For example, while it may be difficult for a person addicted to cigarettes to quit smoking overnight, it may be more manageable to cut down on the amount they smoke in a day, or identify certain situations in which they are told to avoid smoking. Over time, more situations can be eliminated or the number can be reduced to the point where their addiction is overcome. Each step along this process would be referred to as a successive approximation in shaping process.

The final step in the behavioral consultation process is problem evaluation. This involves the consultee returning to the counselor to update them on the progress of the client. They inform the consultant of the results of the implemented plan, either continuing discussing and problem solving, or terminating the consulting relationship as is necessary.

Group Counseling

A role or function that counselors may also take on is that of a leader in group counseling. In some cases, counselors will find that they simply do not have time to counsel individually with all of the clients that they wish to help. In cases such as this, a group counseling model may be adopted. Group counseling may also be a deliberate choice based on the needs of a specific client or category of clients. In any case, group counseling is distinct from individual counseling, and requires consideration of a number of concerns which are not raised in individual counseling.

For example, the number of structural decisions that must be made with regards to group counseling is extensive. The counselor must determine the essential details of when, where, and under what contexts the group will meet. They must also consider structural elements involving considerations of group size, counseling duration, and procedures that will be followed in communication. In addition, determinations must be made as to whether the counseling will involve homogenous or heterogeneous groups, whether the group will be open or closed, and whether to involve co-counselors among other concerns. All of these concerns are either implied or irrelevant in individual counseling, but are necessary when group situations are considered.

To expand on these decisions further, one of the considerations that counselors must make is whether to work with homogenous or heterogeneous groups. Homogenous groups involve situations when the participants involved are all people with similar struggles or situations. In many cases the members of the group will have separate lives and be unacquainted prior to the therapy. Rather, they will likely develop a bond through the therapy experience. For example, a homogenous group could be all adolescents struggling with eating disorders, or all middle aged individuals with anger management problems. Heterogeneous groups in group therapy are groups of very different individuals who are coming engaging in counseling with the desire to express or reconcile their concerns in some way. For example, marriage counseling and family counseling could be considered a form of heterogeneous group therapy.

Another determination that counselors must make in group therapy is whether the group will be open or closed. Open groups allow members to join and leave at will. Open groups allow the group to evolve continually, with members coming and going as their life situations change. It also creates a dynamic environment and allows a greater number of individuals to receive counseling. However, there are also inherent difficulties with open groups because it may make members feel uncomfortable and cause them to struggle with open discussion as a result of the continually changing circumstances. Open groups contrast with closed groups which remain the same throughout the counseling process.

Finally, the last of the decisions which counselor must consider regarding group therapy relates to the involvement of co-leaders. In some instances, group therapy sessions may be mediated by multiple co-leaders as opposed to a single leader. This co-leadership model has a number of different benefits for the group therapy session. One such benefit is that it typically helps increase communication and effectiveness of therapy. If a group is large it is easy for some members to slip between the cracks. The presence of multiple co-leaders allows increased interaction of the group members with the leaders and with each other. Put most simply, two heads are better than one.

The co-leadership model also allows for an additional authority figure to consider the group dynamic and help each individual and the group as a whole. A second leader can add a unique perspective which is an added benefit to the members of a group, especially in cases where the specific opinions of the leaders may differ. It effectively results in a built-in consultant. This can be beneficial because all clients will be different. They will both prefer different styles and respond to different methods. Another benefit of co-therapy is that when an emergency arises for one of the leaders, the session doesn't necessarily have to be canceled, so it creates a more stable treatment pattern for the group members.

A third important benefit of using the co-leadership model is that it creates a sort of role model relationships for the group members to look up to. Many individuals who enter into group therapy have issues in their relationships with others (e.g., marital problems, anger management, social issues, etc.). Seeing a positive relationship between group leaders can provide an example to the members.

However, though there are many benefits of the co-leadership model, there are also some cautions associated with it. For example, co-leaders should avoid creating a sense of power struggle. A power struggle relationship can be detrimental to the therapy. Creating a relationship in which one leader is superior tends to mitigate the opinions of the second leader in the eyes of group members. When leaders have incompatible styles, therapy can stagnate and be harmful to the members.

In a more general sense, numerous benefits exist in group counseling because it creates a safe, open environment through which clients can communicate. For instance, one benefit is that typically in a group therapy setting, different clients will be at different stages in their progression. Those who are just beginning can be encouraged by those who have progressed, and those who have progressed can see that they are improving. Another benefit of group therapy is that it allows individuals to see that they are not the only ones who struggle with a problem, and it can impart a sense of community and support. Because clients are all facing similar difficulties they can give one another suggestions, convey true empathy for each other's difficulties, and help one another recognize destructive patterns or situations that should be avoided. The most important element of group therapy is that all members are able to openly share their feelings. This can help the client to achieve a feeling of peace and relief about the situations that they are struggling with.

Family Therapy

For most individuals, the family situation is one of the most important elements of their life, whether for good or bad. Even in individual therapy it is generally accepted that involving an individual's family in the counseling process is beneficial. This is true on the positive end of the spectrum (in which case the family becomes a network of support and encouragement for the individual), and on the negative end (in which case it is necessary to show the family members how their actions are harmful and should be changed). When an entire family is involved in the counseling process, and is treated as a complete unit rather than as a group of individuals, this is referred to as family counseling. For example, in family therapy, the counselor may refuse to even hold sessions unless all of the members of the family are present.

The primary focus of family therapy is to improve relations within a family. The primary objective of the therapist in family therapy is to understand the interactions that occur between people, rather than analyzing the actions or conflicts within a specific individual. Family therapists also tend to be less focused on specific or individual causes of conflicts, and more interested in the bigger picture of how the individuals react to each other. A family systems therapist may consider transgenerational issues, or try to determine how family interactions are resulting in a client's difficulties.

Virginia Satir

One of the foremost theorists in the development of family therapy was **Virginia Satir.** Satir's theories were highly humanistic and experiential. Satir believed that families operated around a delicate balance of patterns in communication and distributions of power. Another important assumption of Satir's is that families operated as a whole. Any problems or unbalances in the life of one member of the family will impact the functioning of the family in its entirety. Therefore, she strongly advocated the need to consider and treat entire families to diagnose and reduce problems.

The balance of power and responsibilities was an important focus of Satir's. She spent a great deal of time studying the triadic relationships which develop within a family setting; namely, the relationship between a mother, a father, and a child. According to Satir, when an imbalance developed between parents, the burden was often shifted to the child resulting in coping and functioning difficulties for that child. Therefore, mending the relationship of the parents to restore a healthy balance of power, or simply working with the family to adjust to the new status quo, would improve the psychological health of the family as a whole.

This triadic relationship was not the only relationship that Satir focused her theories on. Satir also considered the impact of communication patterns that existed within the family as a whole. According to Satir, there are four types of dysfunctional communicators within a family. These are the distractor, the computer, the placator, and the blamer. The distractor holds to the mindset that the best way to deal with conflict or difficult situations is to distract from the situation. This can be with facial expressions, physical distancing, changing the subject or other tactics. The computer becomes mechanistic when facing difficult communication situations. They remove themselves mentally and emotionally from situations. The placator is willing to agree with anyone and anything to avoid conflict. Finally, the blamer is unwilling to take responsibility and is continually putting the blame for communication and other problems on other members of the family. Each of these roles reduces the effectiveness of communication and therefore causes problems in the functioning of the family as a whole. It is the responsibility of the therapist to identify and then help to eliminate these practices within families.

In helping families and individuals either move through situations of changing status quo, or in encouraging changes in how family members interact with each other, Satir identified a **five stage progression** that occurs when change is confronted.

The first stage is referred to as a stage of **late status quo.** The status quo describes the current state of the family relationship. This could include how the family currently interacts with each other, and the basic practices and beliefs at work within the family. At this point the family relationship is stable, but not at a desired functioning level. A counselor working with a family in this stage will identify problematic interaction patterns, and seek the individuals in the family to look for alternative interaction patterns.

The second stage of the change process is referred to as **resistance.** In this stage some sort of foreign element is introduced into the family situation. This could be a minor change in the life or schedule of a single family member, or a major change in the family such as death or divorce.

The foreign element could also include conscious attempts by some member so of the family to change or oppose the status quo. In any case, the family is forced to confront something that upsets the tenuous balance that existed in the late status quo stage. The natural response is to resist the foreign element, and strive to maintain the status quo, resulting in minimal change in the overall function of the family. The role of the counselor at this stage is to help the members open up and accept the change.

Satir classified the third stage of the change process as the **chaos stage.** At this point the foreign element can no longer be suppressed and functioning level plummets as the family is forced to begin adjusting to the change. A number of different reactions occur in the chaos phase. For some, it is seen as a tragic death of the old status quo. Old reactions and patterns of behavior are ineffective and this results in a state of confusion and disarray within the family as new patterns of behavior and interaction must be formed. Individual family members will feel unbalanced and will likely have difficulty trusting or interacting with each other.

However, another possible reaction to the chaos phase is passivity. Rather than handle the problem proactively they will essentially just watch and wait as things unravel. Whatever the particular reaction may be, it is the role of the counselor at this point to help clients acknowledge their feelings (fear, discomfort, anger, etc.) and help them work to create a safe and open environment in which to grow and establish a new and better system.

After some time has passed in the chaos stage, **a transforming idea** will emerge. This transforming idea is essentially a realization that members come to which pulls them, at least initially, out of a state of chaos and enables them to begin restructuring the family relationship in a healthier manner. Essentially, the transforming idea involves the family realizing that the changes can and will be a benefit in the long run. However, the transforming idea is rarely a permanent fix.

Rather, it spurs the family into the fourth stage of the change process – integration. In the integration phase, the family acts on the transforming idea and begins to create and use new patterns of interaction and relationships. The role of the counselor in this phase is primarily a supportive one. Counselors need to be aware of what is happening in the family to ensure that the initial effects of the transforming idea to not die out if family members become discouraged as the original motivation dies out. They will offer encouragement and suggest coping strategies.

The final stage of the change process is referred to as **new status quo**. At this point, new interaction patterns and relationships have been established and the result is stability at a higher, healthier level of functioning. Family members will have assimilated to the foreign element and will begin to become comfortable with the new status quo. Here it is the role of the counselor to offer additional support and encouragement. Satir felt that maturity, developing self-confidence, and good communication were the most important elements in assuring functional family situations.

Murray Bowen

Another important theorist in family therapy is Murray Bowen. Bowen's interest in counseling can be traced to the time when he was working as a surgeon in World War II. After a few years of active duty he came to the conclusion that psychiatry and mental illness was a more pressing need than surgery. So, he began to study schizophrenia. His interest turned to family therapy as he began to incorporate the mothers in the treatment of schizophrenic individuals, and began to theorize about the role of family in individual development.

Like Virginia Satir, Bowen took a systems approach to family therapy (i.e., he believed that it was important to study the family as a whole unit, rather than try to isolate problems within individuals). Bowen's theories can be classified into a few major interlocking principles: differentiation of self, triangles, nuclear family emotional systems, family projection process, emotional cutoff, multigenerational transmission process, sibling position.

The concept of differentiation of self was an important element of Bowen's study of schizophrenia which he then applied to family systems therapy as a whole. This element relates to an individual's ability to distinguish their feelings and beliefs from the beliefs of those around them and from intellectual processes. If there is a low level of differentiation among family members, it can lead to emotional fusion. In a state of emotional fusion no distinction or balance between emotions and feelings, and individuals will act only for what seems best at the time.

This creates a tenuous situation which lends itself to rash actions. When emotional fusion occurs, individuals do not reason through situations; rather, they submit to whatever they perceive is demanded of them. They are highly dependent on approval from others and prone to stress related problems. Those who are differentiated, by contrast, do retain a strong emotional attachment to their family; however, they differ from those in a state of emotional fusion because they are able to distinguish their needs, wants, and opinions from those of the larger group. This allows them to reason through situations and come to conclusions about what course of action will be most beneficial to the group as a whole.

Also similar to Satir's theories, Bowen considered the role of triangular relationships to be an important element of family interaction. According to Bowen, when two members of a family are experiencing tension, they pull in the third person to dilute anxiety. Bowen believed this to be the most basic and necessary structural unit of a family; however, it also places the third member in a possibly vulnerable and tenuous position.

The third potential source of difficulties in the family that Bowen identified relates to emotional systems that develop in nuclear families as a whole. He identified four different systems which develop that lead to functional problems that can extend across generations and subsets within the nuclear family. They are marital problems (i.e., relational problems between the parents in a family), problematic emotional functioning, functional impairment, and emotional fusion.

Family projection is the fourth process which Bowen identified as a potential problem source. In a general sense, projection refers to any situation in which a person attributes their own negative feelings to others. In family situations this can occur in parents (e.g., blaming children's bad attitudes for their own frustrations), between siblings (e.g., blaming a sibling's uncooperative nature for fights), or in numerous other contexts. Projection can be a great cause of anxiety and dysfunction in family situations.

Another problem Bowen identified is emotional cutoff. Cutoff occurs when a member of a family feels unable to form meaningful relationships with others. They essentially cut themselves off emotionally from the other members of the family entirely. While this is often adopted as a coping or stress-reducing mechanism, it often results in higher stress levels overall. This is because it disrupts the functioning of the family system as it leaves the family incomplete, and impairs the ability of all the other members to form meaningful relationships.

According to Bowen, problems can also develop within families as a result of multigenerational transmission processes. This refers to situations in which tensions, anxieties, or problems are passed across generations. Multigenerational transmission is often a combined result of projection and triangulation. That is, projection from parent to child within a triangular relationship will result in transmission over multiple generations with time. Because of this problem, Bowen was known for looking at least three generations back in a family for patterns of behavior when a client presented a problem.

The final major element to which Bowen ascribed a potential for causing family difficulties was sibling positions. Bowen believed that generalized traits could be ascribed to different relative positions within the family. For example, eldest children tend to be more leadership oriented and responsible, whereas younger children tend to be more dependent. Bowen was interested in studying the role that triangular relationships played in sibling position.

In terms of applying Bowen's theories to family therapy, Bowen stressed a process which involved first educating clients about the dysfunctions that existed within their family relationship (be it triangulation problems, differentiation problems, cutoff, etc.), in order to reduce anxiety levels about the problem.

Once this has been accomplished, the next step is to begin increasing levels of differentiation in family members, followed by increasing levels of differentiation from family origin (the first part of the differentiation process, then, effectively targets currently operating problems, whereas the second part targets multigenerational transmission issues).

The specific role of the counselor throughout the process is to encourage individuals to take responsibility to change dysfunctional situations, while still remaining differentiated from clients. Because of the enormous amount of involvement required by family therapy, it can be easy for counselors to either become overwhelmed or begin to take on a position of responsibility. Bowen emphasized the need for counselors to encourage responsibility within the family.

Triangulation

Conflict is an aspect of life that at some time or another that everyone must learn how to deal with. Triangulation is a common and destructive way in which many people deal with stressful situations and conflicts. Triangulation occurs when an individual vents to a third party about a conflict with another person. For example, triangulation is common in family relationships where a child might complain about another sibling or friend to their parent, a parent complains to a child about their other parent, or a spouse may complain about marital problems to their own parent. Most often people are not looking for answers when they engage in triangulation.

Rather, they seek the relief of anxiety that comes from venting to another person. The reason that triangulation can be so destructive is that it is temporary. No problems are actually solved, and in many cases they are simply made worse. Communication is vital in repairing a conflict, and triangulation prevents that. Furthermore, triangulation often places anxiety and pressure on the third individual who feels their loyalty is being pulled in multiple directions.

Advocacy

A final important issue regarding the roles and functions of a counselor is the concept of advocacy. Defined in general terms, an advocate is anyone who argues a point for another person or speaks in favor of an idea. Though the term is typically thought of in terms of legal proceedings, this is essentially exactly what an advocate does in counseling as well. With time advocacy is becoming an ever more important and encouraged element of counseling.

One form that advocacy takes in counseling is advocacy through the actions of the friends and family of a client. Advocates are people who care about an individual, and who help them through their counseling process. An advocate may encourage an individual to seek counseling, and could even attend sessions with them to support them. They would be there for them when they are having struggles, and encourage them through the counseling process. Being an effective advocate requires an awareness of the individual's struggles and specific situations, and some basic knowledge and skills which enable them to be of help.

Even more important than these types of advocates is the counselor's role as the client's advocate. Counselors can advocate for their clients on a number of different levels, ranging from an individual sphere, to a systematic sphere, to the public or community sphere. The counselor's role as an advocate becomes relevant when a counselor either discovers or becomes aware of barriers in the life of their client which are hindering their progress. Advocacy is the process by which a counselor works to remove these barriers for their client. It is important to recognize, however, the delicate balance which exists between being a necessary advocate in facilitating improvement, and trying to solve the client's problems for them, which hinders their progression.

There are three different elements which a counselor must develop to be most effective as an advocate: disposition, knowledge, and skills. The element of disposition refers to a general willingness and ability to act as an advocate for clients. Counselors should be sympathetic and aware of the needs of their clients to an extent that they can recognize areas in which advocacy may be necessary. In addition to these basic personal attributes, a counselor must also be willing to act in their client's interest, whatever that may involve (within reasonable ethical, legal, and professional bounds).

The second element, knowledge, involves an incorporation of both the avenues through which advocacy can take place and knowledge of techniques involves with advocacy. To act effectively as an advocate, a counselor needs to be aware of the resources and programs available to their clients. For example, substance abuse counselors should be aware of self-help groups and programs within the area. Similarly, mental health counselors should be aware of the research, institutes, agencies, and community groups involved with the difficulties that their clients face.

The third element, skills, is more directly concerned with the ability of the counselor to act as an advocate. Skills that counselors should develop include communication skills, organizational skills, the ability to recognize when their clients are facing problems, and other related skills. Communication and organization skills will aid counselors when working with others to help remove barriers for clients, as well as in helping the client overcome difficulties themselves. Collaborative skills will help counselors to build a network from which to base their advocacy efforts for clients.

Once a counselor has developed competency in advocating for clients, there are a number of different levels at which counselors can begin to advocate. The level or levels at which the counselor works will depend on their abilities and on the individual needs of clients. Advocacy begins at an individual level. This most fundamental level of advocacy involves examining the situations directly creating barriers for the client, and working to remove those barriers. One of the most common barriers faced by individuals is a lack of access to needed resources. For example, a client addicted to drugs may need information regarding self-help groups to help them more effectively overcome their addiction.

The next level which a counselor may advocate at is the system or community level. Advocacy at this level involves identifying systematic factors which are causing problems for the client. The counselor is primarily an ally of the client in combating these factors. Some of the actions which counselors may take at this level include making organizations aware of the barriers that they are creating for the client and others, and alerting the public in general to the problems caused by an organization. Changing the status quo that exists in a community is the main goal of this type of advocacy. In a school counselor setting, advocacy at the individual level could involve negotiating with administrators to arrange a student's schedule to be more conducive to medical, spiritual, or academic needs.

The third and highest level that counselors advocate at is the public or political level. This form of advocacy involves combating widespread matters requiring advocacy in the community or world as a whole. For example, environmental concerns, discriminatory issues, and societal concerns would all be addressed at this level. Because this form of advocacy addresses societal needs as a whole, they therefore advocate for both their clients and the general public simultaneously.

Counseling Relationship

When it comes to counseling, the most important aspect in determining the success and improvement of the client is the relationship that exists between the counselor and client. Simply put, no other factor has shown so consistently to have a major impact on the success of the counseling process. Because of this, it is extremely important to understand the different aspects which can affect the balance and health of this relationship. By understanding these factors the counseling relationship can be made most effective and useful. There are three overarching factors to consider relating to the counselor that impact this relationship: who the counselor is, what the counselor knows, and what the counselor does.

Who the counselor is refers to the personal qualities of the counselor. Just as every person is different, with their own individual character traits, personalities, flaws, and expertise, every counselor will be unique. This is a benefit to counseling as a profession because it enables clients to find a counselor whose style is most suited to them personally. However, there are a number of traits that it is advisable for all counselors to cultivate which will allow them to be more effective in their work.

One of the most important qualities for a counselor to develop is an ability to listen. By listening intently to clients, the counselor conveys genuine concern which is instrumental in building a relationship with the client and progressing with the counseling process. Also, if a counselor does not know how to listen effectively, they will not be able to understand what their clients are telling them.

Trust

A quality that it is important for a counselor to develop is trust. In many cases the only interactions which the counselor will have with their clients are in scheduled meetings. This means that the counselor must develop a characteristic trust of their clients and the things that they tell them. Although it is the role of the counselor to give guidance and advice, the counselor should be open to the judgments or interpretations that a client offers as well (i.e., do not categorically discount anything that a client says). Counseling is an interactive process and failure to trust the client will severely handicap the relationship.

Verbal and Nonverbal Behavior

A counselor can convey that they are listening through both their verbal and nonverbal actions. Most commonly listening is conveyed through verbal methods when a counselor comments on things the client says. They may make a comment or ask for clarification or additional information. Restating or paraphrasing what the client says (or repeating back to them with different wording), commenting or reflecting on the emotional implications of what the client has said, or even a simple summary of what has been discussed during a session are all ways that a counselor can verbally convey that they listen.

Nonverbal listening behaviors are also important elements in conveying interest, concern, and competence. Effective nonverbal listening begins with facing the client squarely. This helps to show that your attention in focused on them. Directing your attention towards them with your posture by facing them conveys involvement in the conversation. Often, leaning slightly towards the client can be effective in conveying involvement and interest in what they are saying.

Maintaining eye contact is also important in conversation involvement. Not meeting a person's eyes is generally interpreted either as shame, boredom, or disinterest. Therefore, failing to do so will likely make the client feel unimportant, embarrassed, awkward, or angry. In any case, it will be detrimental to the relationship and make the counseling less effective and productive overall.

Personality and Characteristics of Counselors

An important quality for a counselor to cultivate is an acceptance of an individual's ability to change. This is clearly a foundational belief of counseling as without this basic understanding there would be no point to the counseling process. A desire to motivate and help the client in their process of becoming a more healthy and happy individual is key to building an effective counseling relationship.

Counselors should also strive to develop a generally open personality. This does not mean that they should be inconsistent or indecisive, but rather that they should be accepting and personable. In some ways this goes along with accepting that people can change. It can involve showing that although a client's past mistakes must be acknowledged to allow future growth, they do not result in a negative or judgmental opinion in the counselor. Cultivating openness and exhibiting a non-judgmental character allows clients to be more free and trusting towards their counselor.

In addition to being non-judgmental of past mistakes, having an open personality can also extend to accepting clients the way that they are. The natural tendency is for a counselor, or any person, to feel most interactive, comfortable, and amiable towards people that they are similar to. It is important that a counselor break out of this natural tendency and is caring and personable in all situations that they encounter. Doing this requires a counselor to explore themselves and their own tendencies to reveal patterns in their interactions, and to be sure that they are acting appropriately in every situation. A counselor should give the same, high-quality treatment to every client that they have, regardless of any personal differences that they may have.

A degree of selflessness is also an important characteristic for a counselor to possess. One of the reasons that people go to counselors for guidance, as opposed to merely referring to friends or family, is that the relationship is non-reciprocal. That is, excluding pay, a counselor does not expect anything from their clients. While a person may feel uncomfortable speaking with friends and family who have their own worries and concerns, it is a counselor's responsibility to be there for them and sincerely work to help them find the best solutions to their struggles.

It is therefore necessary that a counselor is able to keep the focus on the needs and concerns of the client, and to focus on them. Counselors should remember; however, that they need to work through problems with the client, rather than thinking for them or making decisions for them. Ultimate responsibility for making decisions and following through with them lies with the client. The counselor should be encouraging and thoughtful as the client navigates through this process.

Another personal quality that counselors should strive to develop is a healthy balance between consistent, dependent behavior and flexibility. Not only does reliability have courtesy implications (showing up for scheduled meetings with clients and following through with any commitments), it can also be extremely important to the treatment process. Some clients may need a structured environment with clear expectations in order to flourish. This doesn't mean that everything should be laid out and monitored, however. A certain degree of spontaneity is also a healthy practice.

A good counselor should also have self-confidence. They should be secure with themselves and their abilities. If a counselor does not feel confident in their knowledge and ability to help a client, then they will be less effective in guiding them. Confidence allows a counselor to be energetic, accepting, and creative – all of which are important aspects of counseling. Also, if a counselor is not confident in their abilities, then their clients won't feel confident in themselves either. This makes confidence an important trait for a counselor to develop.

An effective counselor will also be a good leader. They will be able to not only keep sessions moving in productive directions, but also effectively encourage and guide clients in their growth. The trick to effective leading is remembering that it is the client who needs to be making the decisions, not the counselor. The counselor may have the client reflect on their feelings, consider different angles to their problems, or encourage them to consider a problem more deeply. It is important that a counselor gives balanced considerations to client's feelings, physical responses, and intellectual responses to situations.

While it is good to understand the qualities which a counselor should strive to develop, counselors should also be on guard against a number of unhelpful behaviors which they may fall into. For example, while counselors should seek to advise and help their clients, they should be wary of falling into a pattern of lecturing. An important aspect of effective counseling is that the client should learn how make wiser decisions for themselves. A good counselor will guide clients and teach them to reason for themselves and allow them to make decisions.

Another unhelpful pattern to be wary of is excessive storytelling. While communication and familiarity are important between a counselor and client, the focus of counseling should be on the client, not the counselor. Short anecdotes may occasionally be helpful in illustrating a point, but storytelling can take away from the allotted time for the session and many clients may consider stories a waste of time that are not applicable to them.

The next factor, what the counselor knows, refers to the training which a counselor receives to qualify them to counsel patients. Because the field of psychology and counseling is so diverse, there are a number of educational pathways for a person to take in becoming a counselor. A person who desires to become a counselor should consider what their specific interests are in determining what pathway to take.

In any case, there are some general things that all counselors and therapists must learn. For example, knowledge about theories, models, and types of personalities is common to all types of counseling. Knowledge of different theories about human development is also a foundational knowledge. The study of personalities and development is important in any counseling field because working with different individuals of varied personalities is the basis of the profession. In addition, understanding how people develop and react in different situations is important in helping them grow and better understand themselves.

Another factor in what the counselor knows relates to an understanding of the various therapeutic models. Throughout the course of history a number of psychological models and theories have developed. These include the psychoanalytic model, psychodynamic theory, phenomenological perspective, person-centered theory, behavioral models and many other approaches to name a few (these will be discussed in a later section). Counselors must become familiar with these various models so that they have a direction in their methods and an understanding of the process of counseling.

A counselor should also have knowledge of various assessment techniques and intervention strategies. Because one of the primary responsibilities of the counselor relates to working with clients and helping them through their difficulties, it is important that they are able to employ various techniques in assessing the problem. Because every client and situation is different, a counselor may be required to use various methods throughout their career, and even their day. The ability to effectively determine the root causes of the difficulties which clients are struggling with is essential in helping them overcome these difficulties. This requires an aptitude in gathering information, such as through questioning and careful consideration of verbal and nonverbal behavior and synthesizing it to come to a valid conclusion.

For example, a counselor may make effective use of open-ended and close-ended questions in discussions with clients. Open-ended questions are appropriate when a counselor wants a longer, narrative, or elaborate answer to a question. They allow the client to more freely express themselves and give the counselor a chance to get to know more about their personalities. Close-ended questions are appropriate when a counselor wants to illicit decisiveness, or simply wants a specific question asked. In situations where the counselor wishes to direct the flow of the conversation these types of questions are appropriate because they allow only a yes or no response from the client.

The knowledge and qualifications that a counselor has can affect the counseling relationship because it will affect how the counseling progresses. Each counselor will have their own unique technique and style when it comes to interacting with clients, and it is important to be aware of this fact. Clients should choose counselors with whom they feel comfortable interacting, and who they trust. Counselors should strive to be aware of how their style can possibly be modified or fit to the needs of a certain client to be most helpful to them. A well-rounded understanding of various techniques and theories is important for a counselor to have in order to know how to most effectively guide their clients.

The third factor to consider affecting the counseling relationship is what the counselor does. Clearly this factor will be heavily influenced by each of the preceding two factors (who they are and what they know). The range of responsibilities that the counselor has can be large. For example, many therapeutic theories involve the counselor in teaching the client. This could include assigning them tasks to complete such as reading a book that relates to their difficulties, or coaching them to employ more productive thought processes.

An important tool that counselors can use with clients is goal setting. Setting goals with clients promotes improvement and gives the counseling a direction. Effective goals should be specific, measurable, attainable, and have time constraints. They should be relevant to the behaviors which the client wishes to improve, and mutually agreed upon by both the counselor and the client (again emphasizing that it is the client's responsibility to make decisions and carry through with them).

Another action which counselors can take which will affect their relationship with their client is called **intervention.** In non-counseling situations, an intervention refers to a situation in which friends and family confront an individual about a difficult, dangerous, or negative behavior that they feel needs to be addressed. An intervention in a counseling situation, then, is when the counselor involves friends and family in the counseling processes. This can affect the relationship that the counselor and client have because it pulls additional people into the relationship. A client may feel either touched or hurt by the counselor's actions, so it is important that the counselor is aware of their client's preferences and needs before doing so.

In addition to these three aspects (who the counselor is, what they know, and what they do), which relate specific to the counselor, there are a number of other factors and considerations to acknowledge in considering the counseling relationship. For example, understanding proper usage of verbal and nonverbal behavior can be an important element of the counseling relationship.

 Communication

Verbal communication refers to the basic conversation which takes place during counseling. Discussions between counselor and client, the process of asking and answer questions, paraphrasing, and explaining feelings are all examples of verbal communications which may take place in counseling. Verbal communication is the most basic and essential way that people interact with one another, and is the primary method of communicating information, asking for help, entertainment and persuasion.

Where verbal communication is involved it is important to understand the implications of paralanguage. **Paralanguage** refers to communication that occurs indirectly through verbal communication. It includes aspects of verbalized language such as pitch, tone, and tempo of voice. For example, regardless of what a person is saying, tone is an important element to properly understanding meaning. Tone can convey severity, light-heartedness, sarcasm, or any number of other emotions. This is similarly true for pitch, tempo, inflections, and volume.

Verbal communication is essentially the basis of all communication. However, just as important to effective communication are the nonverbal communications which occur. In fact, when people perceive a difference between the verbal and nonverbal signals that a person manifests, their reactions and opinions will more likely than not be framed by the nonverbal observations. This makes it very important to understand the types and implications of nonverbal communication.

Nonverbal communication can take on a number of different forms. One of the most basic types of nonverbal communication is the use of body language. Body language can often convey more about what a person is thinking or feeling than their words do. Body language refers to communication factors which relate to physical signals. It includes posture, gestures, expressions, and eye movements. Body language can be both intentional an unintentional.

Intentional body language refers to actions that we take to purposely convey something. For example, when a person is angry and they frown, narrow their eyes, or fold their arms to manifest it. Violence is also a form of intentional body language used to convey anger. Conversely, a concerned expression, open eye contact, and comforting touch are examples of intentional body language which may be used to convey empathy. In each case it was body language, or physical signals, which were used purposefully to communicate in place of words.

Intentional body language can come in a number of forms. Translatable body language describes gestures or movements that have universally accepted and understood meanings. Commonly used gestures or actions would fall under this category. Another classification of body language is affect-display actions which are actions such as facial expressions and gestures which are used to convey emotions.

Intentional body language can be a powerful way to communicate emotions and build positive relationships with clients. However, it is also important to be very conscious of the touching aspect of intentional body language. Although touch can be a powerful tool in creating bonds and conveying empathy and understanding for a client, physical contact continues to become an increasingly difficult and troublesome subject. Counselors should be very careful in their use of touching, and be aware of the client's reactions to ensure that it is not misinterpreted or unwanted in a given situation.

An additional important aspect of body language is unintentional body language. Unintentional body language refers to unconscious or natural movements and signals that people make and which can be important in communication. While expressions and gestures can be used intentionally to convey emotions, often they are made unconsciously. For example, if a person is bored, their eyes will wander. Touching of the face is often considered to be an indicator of a lie. Or, an irritated person may tap their foot or roll their eyes. Learning to pick up on these and other signals can increase a counselor's ability to effectively interpret how their clients feel.

Posture is also an aspect of body language that can be useful in interpreting how an individual feels. Rigid and immobile posture may convey superiority or discomfort in a situation, whereas crouching towards an exit, slouching, or a relaxed posture will each convey something entirely different. It is important to be aware of the implications that posture will have both as it relates to how the client views the counselor and to how the counselor should interpret what the client is saying and feeling.

Nonverbal communication can also extend to areas outside of body language. For example, in some cases when something is not said it can be even more powerful than if something is said. Therefore, understanding how to effectively use silence is a useful tool in therapy. Silence plays an important role in therapy, and can be either a useful tool or a detrimental factor depending on the situation in which it is used.

There can be many benefits to periods of silence during therapy sessions. One of the most common reasons that silence is used by therapists is as a way of communicating empathy, understanding, and acceptance. When used effectively, silence can magnify these feelings between a therapist and client. Silence can also give clients an important chance to collect their thoughts and consider their feelings. Allowing periods of silence to extend beyond what they normally would, therapists may encourage client's in sharing feelings and allow them to better verbalize their emotions. If a therapist continuously interrupts silences, feeling that they are awkward or useless, it could be detrimental to the client and prevent them from truly considering their emotions or opinions.

On the other hand, silence can be harmful in therapy when it is not used appropriately. Although silence may be meant to convey understanding and empathy, for some patients it increases feelings of anxiety and isolation. In situations such as this, the client may perceive the therapist as cold, or consider them to be incompetent. Because of this it is very important that a therapist understand the delicate balance that exists in the use of silence, and cultivates a skill for using it tastefully. Typically, silence is considered to be safest and most effective for proactive or problem oriented clients, whereas it is not used with clients who have severe or deep set emotional issues or disturbances.

An additional type of nonverbal communication which should be considered is communication which is indirect or implicit. For example, the way that a person dresses can be a form of communication. Dressing ostentatiously communicates a different message than dressing in muted colors. In a similar manner dressing casually conveys a different message than dressing formally. How a person presents themselves can be an important method of indirect communication.

Other factors in communication include whether or not a person remembers an appointment or important event. For example, when a husband forgets his anniversary or his wife's birthday, it will likely be interpreted as a sign that he does not consider it an important occurrence. In such an example, although nothing is said or done it is still an important form of communication. Similarly, if a person goes out of their way in order to be at an event or help another individual it indirectly conveys how important it is to them. Indirect communication forms such as these can be combined with other forms of communication reinforce or alter meanings as the case may be.

The Counseling Environment

Research has long shown that environments can have a significant effect on the physical, emotional and psychological well-being of an individual. As such, it is important that counselors and therapists practice good design in their office spaces to maximize the comfort, and eventual improvement, of their patients.

Determining how to design an office can be a difficult task. While every situation may call for specific elements, there are some general guidelines to consider. In terms of decoration, people tend to favor offices decorated with softer elements such as pillows or rugs. Spaces that are cluttered or crowded generally result in lower client opinion. It is also important that the counselor's credentials are displayed. This shows clients that they are in professional hands, and are getting decent care.

Along these same lines, having live plants in the room can add to the atmosphere; however, if there are plants they should be well maintained and lively, so as to avoid creating a depressing or lifeless atmosphere. Having dying plants will make the client question whether the counselor can help them when they can't even keep a plant healthy.

An important consideration of the design of any counseling space is the need to create a sense of privacy. Although clutter makes a space feel uncomfortable, if a space is too open and makes the client feel exposed or on display then it will detract from their ability to share their problems and feelings.

Lighting is also an important consideration in counseling settings, and can be helpful in creating that feeling of privacy. When it comes to lighting, a healthy balance should be maintained between too light and too dark. Although having dark or unlit corners should be avoided, dimmer office spaces also tend to make clients feel more comfortable and safer talking about themselves. Spaces that are brightly lit can come off as imposing and frightening.

Although many people have a notion of counselor's offices in which the client lies on a couch with the counselor sitting over them, this is rarely the case in practice. This setup was used early on by Freud. However, the client-centered model which developed shortly after required face to face interactions and an impression of equality. As a result, today is it much more common to have chairs to sit and converse in. When an office does have couches they are also intended to be sat on, not lain on. One factor to be wary of in selecting furniture is the message that will be sent by it. If a counselor's chair is perceived as nicer, fancier, bigger, more comfortable, or in some other way better than other pieces of furniture, clients may be annoyed or feel as though they are asserting superiority.

Wherever possible, the office should also be a reflection of function. If a counselor works primarily with individuals they will have different furniture considerations than if they work with groups or couples. A counselor should consider the needs and preferences of their clients in organizing the space. However, in addition to considering functional and preferential aspects as they relate to clients, counselors should also consider their own tastes and preferences. They will be spending a significant amount of time in the space, and it is appropriate that the space reflect their style. The trend in counseling spaces currently is an attempt to create a homey, comfortable space. This allows for a certain amount of personalization, such as pictures of family, artwork, or hobby-related items, as long as they don't impose on the comfort of clients.

Another important aspect to consider is noise. When there are many different offices adjacent to each other, a good investment is a white noise maker of some sort. This will cut down both on distracting city noises, and on sounds carrying over between offices. Although it is important to be aware of specific patient needs as some patients will be annoyed by these, many will feel more comfortable in the "quieter" environment and feel like their privacy is more protected.

Empathy

Other major considerations of the counseling relationship include the emotional environment which the counselor creates. Although many personal characteristics that counselors should strive to develop have been mentioned, there are additionally three essential qualities which a counselor must convey to be effective and to create a healthy relationship with clients. These qualities combine with the natural (or developed) personal characteristics in creating a truly open, productive, and effective counseling relationship. The qualities are empathy, authenticity, and confidentiality.

Empathy, in a general sense, describes when one person sees that another person is suffering and they try to better understand them. When a person is empathetic they are able to see things from the perspective of another individual and understand the emotions and difficulties that they are suffering from their point of view. It is characterized by feelings of genuine caring and understanding. It can be described as vicariously feeling another's emotions, without that person needing to explicitly state them. More formally, it is the ability to consider a client's unique phenomenological perspective, and see the world through their eyes.

Empathy is distinct from sympathy in that sympathy is more characterized by a feeling of pity. A sympathetic person will see that another person is suffering and feel bad about it; however, they don't have the same level of a deep and personal understanding of the person's situation. This isn't to say that sympathy is bad – it is characterized by a desire to help the other person – but the two are distinct and, though they are often seen together, it is possible to feel one and not the other. Therefore, it is essential that a therapist is able to truly empathize with clients, rather than simply judge them or pity them, in order to most effectively help them.

An additional inherent qualification of empathy is the ability to communicate it to the client. In other words, empathy consists not only of the ability to see the world as the client does, but also of the ability to show the client that they were understood. This allows a relationship of trust and open communication to build with the client, and to help them feel more confident in confiding their feelings and perceptions.

Empathy exists in two basic forms or levels. These are primary empathy and advanced empathy. Primary empathy is essentially the level that has been described thus far. It is when the counselor listens to what the client has said, interprets it empathetically, and conveys what they are seeing to the client. Advanced empathy takes this a step deeper by exploring any possible underlying motives, emotions, or themes that exist in the situations the client describes. Advanced empathy may involve filling in pieces of the story.

For example, consider a situation in which a client describes a feeling of anger with a friend for having talked bad about them behind their back. At a level of primary empathy the counselor would acknowledge these feelings and share sincerely in the difficulty of the situation for the client. At a level of advanced empathy, the counselor may additionally begin to question if perhaps the anger stems from other emotions, such as a fear that what the friend was saying may be true. In this way, advanced empathy requires a closer relationship with the client and deeper understanding of their psychological state. However, it also allows a greater understanding to emerge, and allows for more effective counseling to occur.

Authenticity

The next quality, authenticity, tends to come naturally along with the concept of empathy, but which should still be addressed. Authenticity, most simply stated, is being genuine and sincere in interactions with others. Authenticity is clearly an important element of counseling because the inability to be authentic will result in a relationship that feels fake or strained. Even if the client does not notice the authenticity of the counselor, it is often considered dishonest and wrong. At the most basic level, a counselor will be less effective and less able to help their clients if they do not feel a genuine caring and understanding for them.

Confidentiality

The final element, confidentiality, is also important in establishing a healthy and productive counseling relationship. Confidentiality is one of the most important aspects of therapy because clients must feel safe in disclosing their personal feelings and opinions for the therapy to be most effective. Confidentiality is essential in building close relationships and maintaining the psychological well-being of the client. A client has the right to feel as though their privacy is being maintained in the things that they share with their counselor, and it is damaging to the relationship and process when it is not. In addition to the fact that confidentiality is essential to ensuring that the client is most comfortable, it is also an important element of basic professionalism.

This does not mean, however, that there are not situations in which it is necessary for a therapist to disclose information which has been revealed to them during counseling. These situations can be difficult to determine, and counselors are often required to exercise professional judgment to make decisions regarding confidentiality. If a matter of confidentiality becomes unclear a counselor may wish to consult a legal professional.

There are a few situations in which it is appropriate for a counselor to disclose information gathered in counseling. In general, any time that a client is a danger to themselves or others is one of these exceptions. For example, relevant information may be disclosed if the patient has threatened the counselor's life in some way. Similarly, information may be disclosed if a counselor has serious reason to believe that the client is considering suicide or may harm themselves in some significant way. Another exception is when the client has been informed that certain information will be used or disclosed in other situations, and they have given their consent. If a client is paying with insurance, they may even request that their information is shared with third parties to ensure that they are fully reimbursed.

In some cases it is even a legal requirement that confidentiality is broken. There are three general situations in which a therapist is not just allowed, but required to disclose confidential information. Essentially, any situation in which it is mandated by law should be reported; i.e., if a client confesses to breaking a law. For example, any situation which involves child abuse (either towards or on behalf of a client) should be reported. Also, if information is an issue in a legal proceeding, a counselor may be ordered to disclose information as evidence.

Confidentiality is just one of the many legal and ethical considerations which come into play as a result of counseling. From both a legal and ethical perspective it is easy for difficult questions to arise about the proper course to take. Because the field of ethics tends to allow a certain amount of subjectivity, there are some cases in which the right course of action is debatable. Many professional organizations will publish a code of ethics which outlines specific guidelines for those in their particular field which can be helpful for anyone who has specific questions. The most widely accepted and used ethical code is published by the American Counseling Association (ACA); however, most organizations also publish their own sets of ethical codes which relate more specifically to certain fields of counseling.

Some guidelines that a counselor can follow in their general practice include being aware of the ethics issues that may come up in specific situations, keeping up-to-date on possible shifts in attitudes about ethics or standard practices, periodically reflecting on different situations to determine what the ethical decision is, and being open to admitting when possible mistakes have been made. Most importantly, a counselor should always keep in mind that their first responsibility is to their client, and ensuring their health and dignity are maintained.

Transference & Countertransference

Transference and countertransference are phenomena that often occur during therapy (in fact, some people argue that they are always present, whether or not they are acknowledged) and involve the emotional structure of the relationship. Transference can most easily be described by comparing it to projection. Projection occurs when a patient takes the feelings that they themselves have, and applies (i.e., projects) them to others. For example, if a client doesn't like their neighbor they may project this feeling to believe that the problem is that their neighbor doesn't like them.

Transference is similar to projection but with some distinctions. It is different from projection because when transference occurs the client takes emotions that they may have associated with another significant individual or situation and unconsciously shifts them to the counselor. Therefore, instead of interpreting an emotion or characteristic of themselves to belong to the counselor, they are transferring characteristics or relationships with other people to the counselor. While projection often occurs as a defense mechanism to help relieve anxiety or guilt, transference is simply a psychological phenomenon in which emotions are redirected. As a result, an emotional structure is created between the counselor and client that is not necessarily reflective of their true relationship.

Transference was first noticed and studied by Freud when a female client threw her arms around him. This event led him to further study why clients may develop a false connection to their counselors. In its early stages, transference was generally used to describe situations in which clients felt an attraction to their counselors, but over time it has come to apply to any range of emotions, positive or negative, which a client may have for their therapist. Feelings of rage, hatred, affection, or treating a therapist like a parent are all emotions that can be associated with transference.

Transference does not necessarily occur only during counseling. It occurs in a variety of ways in everyday situations. For example, if a person interacts with someone who wears the same perfume or cologne as an important individual in their life, they may unconsciously react to that person in similar ways or be predisposed to feel a certain way about them. If the perfume matches their mother's they may have an overt respect for them or if it was an old boyfriend they may feel an attachment to them.

As a more serious example, consider a person who had a strained and confrontational relationship with their father. The result may be that later in life they tend to have similar problems with any male authority figures, and it could interfere in their work, religious, and social interactions. Considering the counseling implications, they would likely be argumentative and difficult during counseling as well. On the opposite end of the spectrum, if they had a loving and respectful relationship with their father, this could also result in transference to the counselor.

Although in some cases transference can lead to complications (such as in the example above), transference can be a useful tool for a therapist in building a trusting relationship with their clients. It is also signals an important element that must be worked on in counseling. This is because, especially in psychotherapy, analyzing transference is useful to a therapist in understanding the client's situations and helping them work through them. The idea behind this is that if the relationship is impactful enough that the client is transferring it to others, there is likely a conflict or difficulty relating to that individual which they need to work through.

From the other end of the relationship, it is also natural for counselors to experience feelings of transference in their relationship with their clients. When this occurs it is referred to as countertransference. While countertransference is often noted in reference to inappropriate relations between counselor and client, its applications are as potentially varied as are those of the client. For example, a counselor may associate a client with a child, friend, or parent with whom they had either a strained or positive relationship.

Because countertransference can affect the productivity of the counseling by distracting from needs of the client, it is important that counselors are highly aware of their own emotions. A counselor should be able to identify feelings of countertransference within themselves, and learn to manage them effectively. If it becomes necessary, they should be willing to seek help from others in dealing with them.

Parataxic distortion is a type of transference. The term was coined by American psychologist Harry Sullivan. It describes situations in which one person views another person in a skewed way based on either their own fictional concept of how the person should be, or their association with another person. In other words, parataxic distortion occurs when the individual transfers beliefs, qualities, or expectations to a person that may not actually embody them. One popular example of this is when people fall in love and refuse to believe that their partner is not perfect. Instead they may see them in an idealized way that reality falls short of. Parataxic distortion can also occur with negative traits. For example, a victim of abuse may associate the negative qualities of their abuser to other individuals who appear like, act like, or associate with them.

Ethics and Legal Issues

Although individual situations will always be unique and varied, there are some ethical concerns which can be considered more generally. One ethical concern that should be addressed regards placing the needs of the client first. A therapist should be aware of any of their own traits, flaws, or unresolved conflicts which may bias them or make them less effective in a particular client situation. It is important to remember the trust which has been placed in them to act in the client's best interests. Where it is possible, a therapist should be willing to consult with colleagues in difficult situations.

Another area of concern in therapy is the matter of informed consent. In other words, the client's decision to take part in various aspects of therapy should be informed, voluntary, and rational. The fact that the client is seeking therapy does not always constitute informed consent, especially considering that many patients may have reduced or impaired mental capacity. A therapist should clearly state, before beginning treatment, what the purpose of the therapy is, what will be expected of the client, what the client can expect from them, and any other issues that may be involved. For example, the issue of informed consent may include discussing matters such as if any videotaping or voice recording will occur, what the treatment schedule will be, how payments and fees work, and any possible alternative treatments for their situation.

Another matter of ethical concern is the possible existence of dual relationships. Whenever a therapist is involved in multiple roles with another individual it is referred to as a dual relationship. Dual relationships can occur in many different situations, such as if a therapist is also a friend to, a family member of, sexually involved with, or a business partner of a person that they are treating. Dual relationships can be concurrent, or happen over the same period of time as the therapy, or they can be sequential, in which case the relationships happens after the other.

Dual relationships of a sexual nature are in almost all situations both unethical and illegal. However, non-sexual dual relationships, such as those involving a therapist counseling friends, family, or community members, need not necessarily be either unethical or illegal. A therapist should consider whether the dual relationship is avoidable or unavoidable. If it is possible the safest approach for the therapist is to avoid dual relationships. This is especially true if the dual relationship has the potential to impair objectivity or effectiveness of treatment, as it may constitute unethical behavior on the part of the therapist to allow it to continue.

Understanding these basic issues regarding ethical matters raises the question of what the proper procedures are when unethical conduct does occur. According to the ACA Code of Ethics, if a counselor becomes aware of a colleague behaving unethically the first step is the try to resolve the issue with that individual (unless this is not possible due to conflict with confidentiality laws). If there is concern that the unethical actions may result in harm for a client it should then be reported to the appropriate state and national committees, licensing boards and other concerned parties.

Additional considerations that counselors need to be aware of are those relating to discrimination. It is important that counselors be aware of the needs of disabled clients, and sensitive to issues involving race. The appropriate behavior in situations regarding racial discrimination tends to be fairly straightforward. Counselors should be aware of any possible racial problems which may emerge, and work to prevent them. Where possible, counselors should also remain attuned to any cultural problems which may affect clients, and be aware of the beliefs and practices of their clients.

A somewhat more complex consideration can be dealing with handicapped individuals. The primary area of concern in this area is simply ensuring that buildings and facilities are accessible to people with a variety of problems.

The Rehabilitation Act of 1973 was an attempt by the US government to more fully enforce the standard of equality set forth in the 14th Amendment to the Constitution by creating specific provisions for disabled individuals. Section 502 of the Act created the Architectural and Transportation Barriers Compliance Board, which has come to be called the Access Board. This board works to ensure that all buildings which are built or maintained using federal funds are accessible to individuals with disabilities. This could include things such as Braille lettering or raised lettering on signs to accommodate those with impaired vision, or ramps and wide hallways for those in wheelchairs, or any other elements which may be necessary.

While Section 502 of the law deals primarily with architectural difficulties a disabled individual may face, Section 504 tends to be the legal basis for any transportation problems. Section 504 requires that necessary accommodations be made for disabled individuals (though it also states that they shouldn't be advantaged in any way either). Section 504 extends to any program or activity that is federally funded. For example, an individual may sue for excessive transportation costs associated with getting to a federal building or attending a program.

The Rehabilitation Act was important, but even more commonly referenced today is the Americans with Disabilities Act, or ADA, which extended these laws to relate to the general public. In other words, the Rehabilitation Act applied only to buildings, activities, programs which received federal funding. This meant that private businesses did not have to accommodate for disabilities unless they chose to do so. The ADA, however, requires that all public buildings (which includes shopping centers, schools, daycares, etc.) be accessible to individuals with disabilities regardless of funding. This law also extends to accessibility in a counseling setting, so it is important that counselors be aware of the possible needs of their clients in designing their office spaces.

 Tarasoff v. University of California

Mental health professionals are placed in a unique position of trust by their patients. Although counselors have a duty to maintain confidentiality of their clients, when it becomes apparent that they are a danger to themselves or others, counselors do have a duty to warn and a duty to protect. These duties were established in the case of Tarasoff University of California.

The case began when Prosenjit Poddar became enamored with Tatiana Tarasoff. When she rejected him, he began to see one of the University therapists named Dr. Moore, who diagnosed him as having a paranoid schizophrenic reaction. When Poddar confessed plans to murder Tarasoff, Dr. Moore warned the police to detain him and began making plans to have Poddar institutionalized. The police briefly detained Poddar and warned him to stay away from Tarasoff, but later that evening he executed his plans and murdered Tarasoff.

Tarasoff's parents sued the school claiming that Dr. Moore owed a duty of protection and should have warned their daughter that she was in danger. The court ruled that because of the special relationship that counselors have with their patients, they do hold a responsibility to warn and protect individuals who are at risk of injury by their patients. Because Dr. Moore knew that Poddar was still at large and posed a danger to Tarasoff, his duty was not complete by simply notifying the police. This ruling extends to all counselors in that it requires that reasonable care is exercised to warn and protect those that are in danger.

 Culture in Counseling

In today's world it is essentially impossible to avoid social and cultural factors. This is true not only in the course of counseling, but also in daily living in general. As a result it is necessary for counselors to be aware of various cultural and social issues in order to both help their clients deal with them, and to ensure that appropriate actions are taken within the counseling framework. Social and cultural issues can be loosely categorized into three overarching areas of concern. They are multicultural issues, such as religion, race, and socioeconomic factors; discrimination issues (other than race), such as gender, disability or age; and societal concerns, such as abuse, violence, and stress.

When it comes to multicultural issues the main areas of concern are religion, race, ethnicity, and socioeconomic factors. Perhaps the most prevalent in the mind of society are those relating to race and ethnicity. In order to better understand these issues an understanding of the terms race, ethnicity, culture, and nationality is necessary. Often the general populous will use these terms interchangeably; however, this can be a cause confusion or offense, so it is important that they are used correctly.

The simplest of these terms to define is nationality. **Nationality** refers to a person's citizenship. It is strictly a geographical and political distinction. A nationality can emerge based on birth or naturalization. Nationality has the potential to change and has little to do with a person's behaviors or characteristics. Because of this it generally has the least value in the counseling setting, except as it may relate to race or ethnicity.

Race, in its most narrow definition, describes a group of people with similar hereditary characteristics. In other words, race is a genetic factor. People of the same race will share a historical lineage, and are characterized by similar physical traits and attributes. In fact, race is almost exclusively used in characterizing physical attributes. Because race is tied to lineage, races are closely associated with geographical groupings (i.e., nationality), but that is not strictly required. Some of the most commonly referenced races include Caucasian (or White), African American (or Black), Asian, Hispanic and American Indian.

The classification of race has become increasingly confused with time. One reason that this occurs is because of the amount of intermarriage between different races. There are essentially no people who can be considered representative of a single racial line. From a scientific standpoint, race also becomes difficult to define because although there are traceable genetic differences between individuals, the theory of evolution claims that all humans evolved from the same source and are homo sapiens. This means that there are just as many similarities as differences between races. Because race can be such a difficult term to work with and define, classification by ethnicity is becoming increasingly useful and common.

Ethnicity is distinct from race in that it can and does describe the geographical and cultural relationships between individuals. In other words, while race is technically a matter of biological classification, ethnicity is a matter of social classification. Because of this, there can be many ethnic groups which are all of the same racial classification. For example, the classification of Asian includes a variety of different ethnic groups. The cultural and social background of a person from Japan will be different than that of a person from Vietnam or from mainland China.

Another way to consider the distinction between an African American individual whose family had been in America for the past two hundred years, and an African American individual who had just recently immigrated to America and gained citizenship. Although the two individuals are of the same historical race, they have entirely different ethnicities because of the difference in their social and cultural backgrounds.

This may become clearer with an understanding of the term culture. Ethnicity is essentially a cultural distinction, so understanding what is encompassed in culture clarifies its meaning. Culture refers to the various social, linguistic, geographical, and behavioral factors which characterize a group of people. In other words, not only does culture encompass both nationality and race, it also considers additional factors about a person. Culture considers the attitudes, values, goals, norms, and beliefs which make a group of people distinct from others. It can also encompass artistic tastes, food styles and preferences, and clothing.

Culture is an essential part of who a person is, and plays a large role in how they interact with others and in how they react to different situations. Due to the fact that there are so many different cultures and backgrounds from which a client can originate, it is important that a therapist be aware of issues regarding multicultural therapy. Multicultural therapy refers to a therapeutic approach which recognizes the differences in cultures, and adjusts to be more accommodating to the circumstances of specific clients.

One of the foremost issues that a therapist must address is the role that their own culture plays in their techniques. It is impossible, and rather inadvisable, that a counselor come to clients with no culture or values at all. Doing so would render them unable to effectively counsel clients. However, it is equally important that a therapist does not allow their own views to overshadow the possibly different cultural views of the client.

Therapy is meant to foster an open environment and help the client learn to express themselves. To do this a therapist must have an understanding of their cultural background, and be able to help them achieve their goals in the context of their culture. This can be difficult because the majority of psychological theories were developed by middle class, white, European and American men, and are therefore highly influenced by the value systems of these cultures. Because of this multicultural therapy is diverse and unique and requires that therapists adequately understand and respect the differences in cultures.

When considering the importance of culture, a counselor needs to acknowledge the influence of the opposing forces of assimilation and acculturation which affect individuals living in the United States of different ethnicities and cultures. The traditional view of American culture is that of the "melting pot." This is the idea that with each new individual and culture that is added to the mix, the American culture as a whole is adapted and altered to create something new and unique. This is the principle of acculturation. Namely, acculturation is when a person adapts their own culture to accommodate elements of a new culture. The process of adaptation is what makes acculturation unique from a state of cultural pluralism. Cultural pluralism occurs when a person or group becomes a subset within a larger culture because they retain their culture.

In contrast to the process of acculturation is the process of assimilation. Assimilation is the tendency for an original culture to be replaced by a new culture. For example, immigrants to the United States may abandon the cultural practices which they grew up with in order to fully adopt American culture. A classic example of an assimilating force in the United States is the public school system. In many ways it forces assimilation simply because teaching is done in English, and the practices and laws regarding behavior are determined within the framework of American culture.

Neither assimilation nor acculturation is inherently bad or degrading forces, they are simply different takes on what can occur when different cultures interact. The extent to which they are detrimental or problematic for a client will depend on the needs and wishes of that specific client. Some people of other cultures may struggle because they desire to assimilate fully into American culture, but feel blocked from doing so by family conflict, racial reasons, language barriers, or other factors. On the other hand, some clients may struggle because they wish to retain their own culture as fully as possible, but feel pressured to assimilate. How these factors are addressed in counseling will therefore depend on the specific circumstances.

Other important considerations for counselors dealing with cultural issues are the effects of stereotyping, racism, and ethnocentrism. Ethnocentrism describes situations in which a person views their own culture or ethnicity as central or the best. A person with an ethnocentric mindset will often view their own culture as dominant and then rank all others in relation to it. While this can be a basis for establishing feelings of patriotism or nationalism, ethnocentrism is generally viewed in a negative context because it supports feelings of disdain, judgment, and discrimination of all who are different. Ethnocentricity will often lead to stereotyping and racism.

Stereotyping simply refers to making over generalized assumptions about a person, usually on a basis of race or appearance. Stereotyping is an often criticized practice because in many cases first impressions of a person are entirely unreliable. Also, treating another person on a basis of racial or cultural stereotypes can be detrimental because it will inhibit the ability to get a complete and true picture of what that person is like and what they believe. Stereotypes can often be offensive and hurtful to those who fall subject to them. Therefore, while it is important for a counselor to have a general understanding of different cultural groups and practices, it is also important for a therapist to remember not to stereotype individuals. Counselors should recognize that each person's situation and opinions will be different and unique.

Racism describes a mindset in which a person believes other races to be inferior to their own. Although the term most directly applies to beliefs of a racial nature, in practice it is often extended to include cultural or ethnic prejudices as well. Racism will often evolve as a result of stereotypical beliefs, which is one reason why it is important to avoid stereotyping. Racism can occur on many different levels, starting with a person's own beliefs and the way that they interact with others, and extending to institutional or cultural factors which involve the systematic treatment of a certain group on a wider scale.

The most blatant forms of racism involve the physical treatment of people of a certain race. For example, the Ku Klux Klan was a racist group which flourished in the United States in the late 1800s. They would dress up, wear masks, and commit violent acts against non-white individuals. In some cases, their acts could even range as severe as outright murder. While violence as a form of racism does still occur today, a more common concern is its psychological effects. Large scale stereotyping can lead to a group feeling subjugated or inferior. This widespread perception of inferiority is a form of discrimination. For example, one common stereotype is that multiracial neighborhoods are the more run-down and dangerous parts of a city. Such stereotypes tend to create a self-perpetuating cycle because of the mindset they create within both the affected populations and onlookers.

Racism can also occur in institutional settings, such as within the workplace. For instance, one way in which racism can occur within a workplace is in firing practices.

This might become an issue if the economy were to take a downturn and a company were forced to lay off a large portion of its employees. If they chose to fire only (or first) those individuals with a certain racial or ethnic background, it would be an example of institutional racism. However, if the company fired employees on a basis of the last employee hired was the first that they fired, or those with the lowest quality reviews or those that went to the least amount of college first, then it would not be considered discriminatory because the system wouldn't inherently favor or harm any particular racial or ethnic group.

From a counseling standpoint, it is important that counselors are both able to help their clients work through situations in which racism may be occurring, and ensure that discrimination does not occur within the actual treatment. Racism does not have to be a conscious act. Stereotypes can be ingrained mindsets that don't necessarily manifest overtly, but merely affect the way that individuals are treated. Counselors should be aware of the ways that such stereotypes may be adversely affecting their ability to treat clients, or their client's lives.

Racial issues are not the only factors which need to be considered in a counseling setting. Multicultural therapy is a branch of therapy which considers a variety of different cultural elements which may come into play in client's lives. Multicultural therapy can additionally focus on issues of religion, and even the specific needs and preferences of different cultural groups. The caution of such treatments is that just as with racial situations, it is important that counselors remember that not all individuals within a culture will necessarily ascribe to the typical patterns of that culture. All individuals are unique, and counselors should be able to understand the unique perspectives and situations of their clients.

Another factor that it is important to be aware of is that in most cases in the United States, minority groups are far less likely to utilize mental health care than are white individuals. Though a predisposition against the use of mental health care programs can stem from a number of factors including gender, age, and the environment a person was raised in, the cultural factors which affect a person's use of mental health care are also important considerations. Understanding the predispositions of a group towards counseling can be helpful in treating them most successfully.

For example, one type of multicultural therapy focuses on the treatment of Asian populations. Within Asian culture there is a traditional distrust and disdain of therapy that must be acknowledged before dealing with patients of this culture. The concept of honor is central to Asian culture, and in many cases seeking mental health care is seen as bringing dishonor or shame. Because of this, great care will often be taken to ensure that problems are kept out of the public eye.

The tendency of shying away from mental or emotional disturbances also results in a higher proportion of somatic (or physical) symptoms among patients, and the tendency to seek and accept treatment of physical problems above those involving mental or emotional issues. Asian individuals will typically consider medical treatment before psychological treatment. This means that in many cases a counselor may need to read between the lines with what the client's described symptoms are to determine possible psychological causes of their difficulties.

With Asian cultures it is also important to understand the significance of passivity and respect. The culture is highly patriarchal, and a strong filial loyalty and interdependent family structure are typical. Assertiveness and independence looked down upon as a result, and a quiet wisdom is viewed with respect. It may be detrimental to an individual of traditional Asian upbringing to try and force them into a more aggressive pattern of living. Conversely, an Asian client may experience difficulty when facing assimilation forces (since independence is valued in American culture) due to a fear of disappointing parents or family.

Another type of multicultural therapy focuses on the treatment of African American populations. In a general sense, African American populations tend to be highly family centered. They tend to be more focused on holistic perspectives, emotions, interdependence, and have a great respect for the elderly. Although there are many similarities between the difficulties faced by African American and white populations, certain difficulties tend to be more pronounced or prevalent among African Americans. Also, the difficulties faced by African Americans have unique cultural and historical origins.

One of the key issues that tends to emerge relative to African American counseling is the relationship between men and women. A heavy historical subjugation and stereotyping of African Americans has created a dynamic which often leads to ineffective communication between African American men and women. Many women additionally experience conflict when confronted with pressure to find a spouse within their own race, juxtaposed with the prevalent stereotype of African American males as lower income and education.

Anxiety, depression, and other stress related difficulties are also common among African American women. In historical context, women in African American families have traditionally been expected to be the source of family strength. This was especially the case during times of discrimination or slavery. The enduring expectation of strength and fortitude results in many African American women feeling discouraged from seeking counseling services, viewing them as a sign of weakness or inadequacy. This perceived need to demonstrate strength and coping skills can be an additional cause of anxiety when it conflicts with the traditional open and community oriented culture.

A number of difficulties accepting the concept of counseling also emerge within the African American culture as a whole, as they do within Asian cultures. As a result of historically discriminative practices, many African American individuals tend to be mistrustful of white counselors (and of the counseling institution as a whole). The majority of counselors continue to be white, and the unavailability of same-race counselors is discouraging for some individuals. Also, because many counseling theories and practices are a product of white cultures they may not adequately address the difficulties faced by African Americans – both in institutional situations and in family or other relational settings.

An understanding of the historical context of the African American family can be useful when considering counseling African American individuals. During the early history of the United States, African American families subjected to slavery were often separated from family members, and were generally discouraged in attempts to maintain extended family bonds. Despite this fact, they often formed strong familial ties both within families and with community members. Familial bonds became especially important during the tumultuous post-Civil War era, and the family continues to be an important unit in African American culture.

The tendency to form strong community bonds can have ambiguous effects. Many African American women will seek aid and advice within their daily social networks, rather than from counseling services. While strong social networks are a beneficial feature of African American culture, it can become detrimental if it discourages individuals from seeking formal counseling who would be more benefited by it.

An additional barrier to African Americans seeking counseling is the financial aspect. Despite laws demanding equality, for various reasons African Americans tend to be on the lower range of incomes in the United States. As a result, counseling is viewed as a luxury that many individuals cannot afford. This is compounded by the high rates of single-parent families among African American populations.

In considering the therapeutic strategies which are most successful for African American clients, a counselor should consider a variety of approaches. Because of the importance of family in the African American culture, family therapy can be a highly successful strategy. However, if this method is used, it is important that the counselor can establish a bond with each member of the family. Also, in situations where family therapy is difficult or inappropriate, basic group therapy techniques can also be used. Group therapy is often the preferred method for adolescents and teens from African American cultures. Alternating between individual, group, and family therapy settings can be a useful way to ensure that an individual is receiving the help that they need.

Incorporating a holistic perspective is also important when interacting with African American clients. African American culture also takes a more holistic view of health, and various aspects such as religion, physical health, and emotional health are all considered important. Things such as prayer (or other religious healing options) and natural remedies are an integral part of African American culture, and should not be discounted by counselors.

A third type of multicultural therapy involves the treatment of Hispanic or Latino populations. (The terms Hispanic and Latino are often used interchangeably; however, Hispanic technically refers to any individual of Spanish origin and is the official government designation, whereas Latino refers more specifically to individuals of Latin American origin. Within these two groups there are even additional classifications by which individuals refer to themselves, such as Chicano or Mexicano for Mexican Americans, and Mestizo for those with Aztec heritage.) Firstly, it is necessary to understand the cultural background of Hispanic populations. The classification of Hispanic is an extremely diverse one, and could potentially describe an individual from any other area in Central or South America, though the most common origins of Hispanics in the United States are Cuba, Puerto Rico, and Mexico. As a result of the diversity in national origins, Hispanic culture itself can be diverse and dynamic.

Other demographic features of Hispanic populations include the fact that they are the fastest growing minority group in the United States, which makes consideration of counseling techniques related to Hispanic populations important. Hispanic populations tend to be highly clustered, with a majority of the population in urban areas in western states. As a result, Hispanics have a strong sense of culture and heritage.

Because of the strong cultural heritage of Hispanics, many counselors are more successful with Hispanic clients when they have direct experience with the culture. Especially when working with younger clients it is important that a counselor have knowledge of the culture, and an understanding of traditional values. The predominant religion within Hispanic populations is Roman Catholic, and church and religion are often seen as a source of strength, aid, and information. A respect for elderly is also characteristic of Hispanic culture, with modesty and hierarchy being important values. Hispanic culture also has a tendency to be fatalistic. In other words, individuals believe in the role of fate, and in many cases feel powerless to alter their situations and look negatively on asking for help.

Language is an additional demographic barrier to consider when counseling Hispanic individuals. Because many Hispanics are recent immigrants to the United States, many (especially of older generations) may speak primarily or only Spanish. As a result, a counselor wishing to work primarily with Hispanic clients will need to be bilingual. If a counselor is not bilingual but has a Hispanic client who struggles with English, it is advisable to find a translator. Forcing a client to attempt to communicate in English could severely reduce their ability to effectively communicate, which will hinder the counseling process. However, a number of concerns do arise when translators become involved in therapy.

One such problem is that the client may feel less willing to disclose information to a translator. Another difficulty is that of finding an adequate translator. The translator should have a sufficient knowledge base of both languages to clearly facilitate communication. Friends or family should not be used as translators unless absolutely necessary, as it could be viewed as disrespectful or a breach of privacy and dignity.

When dealing with Hispanic populations it is important to recognize the importance of familism. Familism refers to the fact that the family is an extremely important unit, and is typically given priority over the needs of the individual. The responsibility of family in supporting one another is taken very seriously, and obligations between family members are strong. Hispanics may often favor some sort of family therapy because it allows that culture of support and responsibility to each other to be recognized more fully. If the client does not feel that they are adequately fulfilling family responsibilities it can be a major barrier to their progress.

An important aspect of family relationships in Hispanic culture is a strong division of responsibilities and classification of gender roles within the family. For males there is an expectation of machismo. Machismo is essentially a masculine pride. It is the expectation that men will be strong, dominant providers and leaders of the family. Alternately, the term describing the roles of women in the family is marianismo. The expectation of marianismo is that of a virtuous, nurturing, and submissive homemaker.

The effects of these traditional expectations in counseling can be viewed from two different angles. On the one hand, families adhering to this traditional structure should be appropriately addressed in counseling situations. For example, in family counseling situations the father should be addressed first as he is the leader of the family. Otherwise he may feel displaced and disrespected. In individual counseling situations it is important that the role of the individual within their family is considered. Asking questions relating to how the individual's family views their situation can be useful in determining both the type and strength of family relationships and the client's role within them.

On the other hand, many families may be struggling to adapt under pressures to assimilate. Because independence is such as important cultural value in the United States, it may result in husbands becoming frustrated by increasing independence in wives, and parents becoming frustrated by increasing independence in children. Women may feel pressured to become more independent, or they may struggle to find an appropriate balance between traditional values and new expectations placed on them. Acknowledging and working through these forces may be an important element in counseling Hispanic individuals. Whatever the case may be for a specific client, it is necessary to determine what their circumstances are for counseling to be the most effective.

One of the groups most caught in the conflict of gender roles and cultural expectations are children. In response to this a technique called cuento therapy has begun to develop and gain popularity. Cuento therapy evolved out of the idea of storytelling (cuento means story in Spanish). Across many cultures, storytelling has been a traditional way for parents to convey morals and values to their children. Therefore, cuento therapy is essentially a preventative method of therapy, which works to convey to children the belief systems which are appropriate for them to exhibit. Cuento therapy involves reading adapted folk stories to the children (in both Spanish and English), and discussing the meanings of the stories with them. For example, a story may be modified from its original form of a rural setting to an urban one, with characters being modified to more directly apply to the everyday situations faced by the children.

Another interesting factor related to Hispanic perceptions of counseling is the practice of curanderismo. The term curanderismo evolves from the Spanish word curar, meaning to cure. It is a form of holistic folk medicine which employs a variety of techniques in the healing process. For example, the techniques can range from herbal remedies, to massage therapy, to the utilization of religious icons. Curanderismo focuses on three different healing platforms: mental, physical, and spiritual.

Curanderismo relates to therapy in the extent that Hispanic individuals may be more inclined to seek help through such traditional methods, or even simply through friends and family, before they seek professional counseling services. Understanding this belief system can also help counselors relate better to clients and be more effective. The basis of multicultural therapy is that practices are altered in order to fit the needs of the client. Therefore, if a client considers their sense of self-health in terms of spirituality or mind-body connection, the counseling should orient itself around that element of the client's life. Whatever the case may be for a specific client, it is important for the counselor to become aware of their situation and difficulties in order to effectively tailor their techniques and allow counseling to be productive.

Different Approaches in Therapy

One of the most fundamental questions that a person can ask regards what makes them the way they are. Although on the surface this seems like it should be a simple question, the enormous complexity of the human mind and human interactions has made it essentially unanswerable in any definitive sense. An equally difficult concern, therefore, regards the root causes of mental health problems. Throughout the course of history psychologists and scientists have worked to generate a greater understanding of factors such as personality and how the mind works. In an attempt to help clients (and to simply gain a greater understanding of the human condition as a whole) many counselors and therapists have developed their own methods for understanding, diagnosing, and solving the problems and struggles which their patients encounter.

Though many counselors end up working within their own unique perspective, the many different theoretical approaches can generally be classified under a number of overarching categories. The basic theoretical approaches which will be discussed in this section are psychodynamic, humanistic, phenomenological, cognitive-behavioral, behavioral, systems, eclectic, and holistic.

Psychodynamic therapy is an important psychological approach which underlies a number of different schools of psychology. Some of the most basic characteristics of psychodynamic theory are the assumption that a person's actions are largely controlled by the subconscious or unconscious mind, and an emphasis on the events that occur early in a person's life. Psychodynamic theories typically capitalize on what are referred to as maladaptive functions of the subconscious. In other words, they identify situations in which the subconscious causes conflicts, anxiety, tension or other difficulties in a person's everyday life. Psychodynamic therapies rely on long-term treatment with a strong relationship between counselor and client. Some of the most prominent psychodynamic theories include psychoanalytic theory, Adlerian counseling, and analytical psychology.

 Psychoanalytic Theory

Possibly the most important psychodynamic theory, and the one from which most others evolved, is the psychoanalytic theory, which was developed by Sigmund Freud in the 1920s and 1930s. Freud is possibly the most well-known name in all of psychology, and his theories were radical for his time. Much of what Freud theorized about dealt with the idea of consciousness.

Consciousness is an awareness. This includes an awareness of external events, which are things that happen outside of your body. Internal events are things that happen inside your body such as internal thoughts about your emotions and body functions. Freud believed the unconscious mind motivates our actions. His analysis of human personality and subconscious drives features three main components - id, ego, and superego. Together, these mechanisms combine to aide us in our decision-making and guide us to become the unique individuals that we all are. Robert Young, a professor with expertise in this area, provided the following information used to understand the id, superego and the ego.

The id contains the psychic content related to the primitive instincts of the body, notably sex and aggression, as well as all psychic material that is inherited and present at birth. It functions entirely according to the pleasure-pain principle, its impulses either seeking immediate fulfillment or settling for a compromise fulfillment

The superego is the ethical component of the personality and provides the moral standards by which the ego operates.

The ego coexists, in psychoanalytic theory; with the id and superego…it is the integrator between the outer and inner worlds, as well as between the id and the superego. The ego gives continuity and consistency to behavior by providing a personal point of reference, which relates the events of the past (retained in memory) and actions of the present and of the future (represented in anticipation and imagination).

Alfred Adler

The next important branch of psychodynamic theories is the Adlerian philosophy. Alfred Adler was a contemporary of Freud who branched off later in his career (for which Freud considered him a traitor) and is famous for founding the field of individual psychology. Individual psychology places an importance on how the individual reacts in society, and how they consider themselves. In individual psychology it is the differences in individuals that are of importance. Alder's theory focuses particularly on the development of individuals in their childhood. He believed that people had generally started a course which would determine their behaviors for the rest of their lives around six years old.

Adlerian philosophy differs from psychoanalytic philosophy in the sense that Adler argued that people are goal-oriented, and that they base their decisions on their conscious goals. This contrasts with Freud's psychoanalytic theory because Freud argued that all decisions were a product of the subconscious mind. Adler's work includes an emphasis on the consideration of factors such as family structures, birth orders and dreams.

Adler's theories also depart from Freud's because he did not consider sexual urges to be the primary motivating factor in an individual's actions. Rather, Adler emphasized the role the individual's perception of superiority and inferiority. He believed that a feeling of inferiority drove people to continually strive for betterment and perfection. While Freud argued that people's motivations were unconscious, Adler considered a person's actions to be conscious and goal-motivated. He believed that people faced three different conflicts in their lives: work, social or family, and love and sexuality. How a person perceives their standing in these different fields will determine how they act or behave. If a person does not effectively master the ability to create meaningful relationships and responsibilities in these areas they are left feeling anxious, unworthy, and alienated.

Counseling based off of Adler's theories consists of the counselor and client forming an open and trusting relationship. The counselor should be respectful and try to understand the patient and their situation better (they may discuss their family situation, dreams they have been having, or early childhood memories). The goal of the counselor is essentially to change the client's belief system. They may explain the flaws in how the client currently feels, and may assign them tasks to help orient them to and reinforce the new system. The objective is to help client move past feelings of inferiority, and create a feeling of equality and usefulness.

There are a number of different strategies which may be employed in Adlerian counseling. For example, reflection refers to a strategy of discussing things that the client has said and analyzing them for deeper meaning. Another strategy is called immediacy and refers to focusing on current events. Active wondering is another strategy which involves posing alternative situations and problems to consider. A counselor may also practice a strategy of confrontation to point out contradictions in the client's words or beliefs and actions. Again, the main goal of these strategies is to help clients move past feelings of inferiority, and help them to establish greater confidence in their lives.

Carl Jung

The third major branch of psychodynamic theory is the analytical perspective which was developed by Carl Jung. Like Adler, Jung also studied under Freud, though his theories tend to contradict Freud's psychoanalytic perspective on a number of points. One large way in which the analytical theory differs from psychoanalysis is its emphasis on events that happen during a person's mid-life. While Freud exclusively emphasized the importance of a person's childhood in development, Jung felt that a person equally influenced by both their past and future.

Another unique feature of the analytical perspective is that it considers two different elements of the unconscious mind: the personal unconscious and the collective unconscious. The personal unconscious is basically just what it sounds like. The personal unconscious is the part of a person's unconscious which reflects their own experiences and inner conflicts. Although the memories of the unconscious mind cannot be accessed, Jung believed they were important in the role of personality and other individualizing factors.

The collective unconscious, on the other hand, is entirely different. The collective unconscious contains a collection of the universal human consciousness which extends from the beginning of the human race. The collective unconscious is manifested through archetypes and can be seen through dreams, art, literature, cultures, and behaviors. According to Jung, it is through an integration of these elements of the unconscious with the conscious mind that is the goal of human life. He refers to this process as individuation.

Humanistic Therapy

Moving on from psychodynamic theories, another important field of psychology consists of the Humanistic and Existential therapies. The basis of humanistic theory is the belief that individuals have the ability to seek personal growth and improve their own lives. Humanistic theory advocates the concept that human beings have an innate desire for growth. Because of this, the main goal of humanistic therapies is to uncover and remove any barriers that are keeping a client from achieving a state of awareness and growth. Humanistic theory is focused on immediate and future situations, with the rationale being that individuals are always changing. What is important is helping the client make their way to a more stable, responsible, and free situation in the future. Some examples of theories which are considered humanistic include person-centered therapy and Gestalt therapy.

Person-centered therapy, or **client-centered therapy**, is probably the most influential field in humanistic theories. The person-centered therapy was developed by psychologist **Carl Rogers.** Person-centered therapy is built off the premise that people are naturally positive, honest and capable of moving forward. The primary role of the counselor, then, is merely to provide a basis of support and understanding from which they can do so. Under the person-centered theory, because people know themselves better than anyone else does they are self-directive, and it is important that the therapist does not take on a role of pushing them in any one direction.

Person-centered therapy takes the view of clients as individuals who are experiencing incongruence. This occurs when their perceptions of who they are and where they are going do not coincide with what they want or think they should be. The goal of therapy, then, is to remove any barriers which are inhibiting this progression, and help the client to feel more empowered and open to their surroundings and situations. It is important to understand that the client is considered the one who brings the change. The client knows what is wrong and knows what they want and need. The role of the counselor is in creating a positive relationship for them to push off of.

The fundamental belief of person-centered theory is that the relationship which is created between the therapist and client is far more important than any knowledge or technique which the therapist has developed. Because the therapist-client relationship is so important, Rogers identified three essentially traits for them to possess: congruence, empathy, and unconditional positive regard.

Congruence, which can also be referred to as genuineness or authenticity, refers to a state of open expression in which the client perceives the therapist as a real person and can connect with them. The idea is that the client is better able to express themselves and trust and communicate with the therapist when they are more genuine and real. Congruence also requires that a therapist possess a sincere interest in the well-being of their clients.

Empathy, in a general sense, describes when one person sees that another person is suffering, and they try to better understand them. When a person is empathetic they are able to see things from the perspective of another individual and understand the emotions and difficulties that they are suffering. It is characterized by feelings of genuine caring and understanding. According to Rogers, it is essential for an effective therapist is able to truly empathize with clients, rather than simply judge them or pity them, in order to most effectively help them.

The third characteristic, unconditional positive regard, refers to a state of lasting, warm, and genuine caring for the client which is not characterized by judgment. The therapist should cultivate an atmosphere in which the client feels a sense of positive regard and empathy regardless of what they do or say. It also requires that they do not feel as though the therapist is classifying their words or actions into categories of good and bad. Rogers argued that although unconditional positive regard may not be possible for all therapists to feel in all situations, without it the therapy would be essentially useless. That is, if a counselor cannot generate a feeling of positive regard for a client, they are not the most effective choice of counselor for that client.

Existential Therapy

Existential theory is rather similar to humanistic theory in the regard that it focuses on the freedom of the individual. Existential therapy is also rooted in immediate situations, although it continues to acknowledge the importance of the past. This approach rejects the claim that people are victims of circumstance, and rather approaches life with the belief that people have the power, for the most part, to be free and happy in their lives.

The primary difference between humanist and existential philosophies is in how they portray the natural human state. Humanist philosophy takes the view that people will naturally progress under the proper conditions. In other words, everyone has potential. Existential theory, on the other hand, advocates the belief that the world has no natural meaning, and that it is up to each individual to create that meaning for themselves.

Existential therapy encourages individuals to recognize the limitations and restrictions in their lives, and to find ways for growth and fulfillment in spite of them. Rather than working to find a cure or solution for an individual's problems, existential therapists work to help them see the ways in which they can become freer in their decisions. Therapists work to help individuals see how their problems may have been a result of their own actions, and help them find ways to overcome the mental perspective of being trapped by their situation. Once the client can see the ways in which their life is restricted, they should then be encouraged in taking the responsibility to make a more positive situation in the future. Therapists work to move their clients from a state of restricted existence, in which they feel trapped and distressed by their situations, to a state in which they feel free and open to life.

Existential therapies are characterized by five basic principles. First, that people have a capacity for self-awareness. The idea behind this principle is that as a person expands their awareness, they open up greater possibilities for themselves. However, it also opens up the possibility for more struggles in life.

The second principle is that people have the freedom and ability to shape their own destiny. Existentialism emphasizes the role of the individual, and encourages individuals in choosing to take control of their own lives and situations. However, it also cautions that consequences are a natural result of choices, and that people must be willing to accept responsibility for their choices.

The third principle of existential therapy relates to the individual's relationship with others. In existential theory it is believed that the individual is in conflict due to the contrasting desire to be accepted and gain approval from others, and the desire to find and pursue their own solutions to problems. Existentialism encourages individuals to pursue their own identities, rather than looking to others to guide their actions. Inherent in this philosophy is the idea that people are ultimately alone, but that experiencing aloneness allows a person to look inward and better themselves.

The fourth principle is an interest in the pursuit for meaning. Different existential therapies focus on important aspects of the pursuit of meaning such as evaluating and releasing (renewing) old values which inhibit the ability to find meaning. Existentialism is also characterized by a concern about feelings of meaninglessness in patients. Helping clients find meaning in life is one of the primary goals of existential therapy.

The fifth important principle in existential therapy is that anxiety is a natural condition of life. Existential theory differentiates between a normal sense of anxiety, which is considered the natural response to challenges and confrontations, and neurotic anxiety. Normal anxiety is healthy and motivates people to progress and change. This anxiety is normal, healthy, and constructive. Neurotic anxiety, on the other hand, is not healthy and should be avoided. Coming to terms with anxiety, and keeping it in healthy proportions, is another important goal of existential therapy.

 Logotherapy

One of the most well-known and influential branches of existential therapy is logotherapy. The practice of logotherapy was developed by a man named Dr. Viktor Frankel. Frankel argued that rather than pleasure, acceptance or superiority, the main drive of an individual is in finding meaning in life. It is from this philosophy that the name originates – "logos" in Greek can be translated as "meaning." Although logotherapy is typically considered primarily an existential philosophy, it has also been called the "Third Viennese School of Psychotherapy." This is because Frankel was from Vienna, as were both Freud and Adler.

The foundation of logotherapy can be summarized in three main points: first, all life has meaning; second, people have a will to meaning; third, people can activate their will to meaning and pursue a better life. The emphasis on the fact that all life has meaning is based on the premise of free will. All humans have freedom to choose. However, logotherapy recognizes that life has limitations and restrictions that an individual is forced to work within. Despite these limitations, Frankel maintained a strong belief that it is the individual's responsibility to shape and determine their life within that inherent framework.

The second point, that people have a will to meaning, refers to the fact that people are able to find a meaning in their life, and that once people know what their purpose is they can deal with any trial that faces them. When people do not have a will to meaning (i.e., when they cannot find purpose in their life) this gives rise to anxiety which can lead to other problems such as anger issues, depression, suicidal tendencies, or addictions. A counselor practicing logotherapy will help clients work through these struggles to help them see the greater meaning in their life, and to find fulfillment through it.

Each person's will to meaning is different and unique. Because of this it is important to not guide clients towards specific meanings, but help them explore their own possibilities. This is not to say, however, that meaning is not real. One of the interesting elements of logotherapy is that Frankel argued that meaning was a sort of objective reality. In other words, meaning is a real and concrete thing, and not a subjective illusion created by a person. This contrasts with many theories which work to merely divert a person's attention away from their difficulties.

Regarding the third principle, that people have the ability to pursue a better life, Frankel believed that there were three ways for people to discover meaning in their lives: by fulfilling a need or doing work, through interactions with others and important life experiences, and through choosing to have a positive attitude in the face of suffering. As a survivor of the Holocaust (Frankel spent three years in a concentration camp), Frankel recognized that both of the first two options could be taken from a person. This is the reason why he placed such a focus on the third options – because it was the one that a person truly has universal control over. He therefore posited that by embracing suffering, and working with the situations that arise in life, a person could attain happiness regardless of situation. This is not to say that Frankel advocated suffering, but that he recognized that often it is unavoidable. In such situations it is irrational to succumb to it (for example, being placed in a concentration camp, the death of a loved one, or other uncontrollable situations).

Logotherapy employs three primary techniques: paradoxical intention, Socratic dialogue, and dereflection. The basis of paradoxical intention relates to the freedom of will. Paradoxical intention, also called self-distancing, is typically applied to patients with compulsive disorders, anxiety, or phobias. It is based on the idea that in many cases these problems become self-fulfilling. That is, a person who is afraid of something only heightens their problem and anxieties because they are expecting it. For example, a person who is afraid of dogs will only make their actual fear worse if they spend all of their time worried about encountering a dog. Frankel used the idea of paradoxical intention to counter this by telling patients to actively seek the thing that they fear.

Socratic dialogue is essentially a self-awareness technique. It involves active, questioning dialogue between counselor and patient. As a person engages in Socratic dialogue they are able to gain a perspective on their situations, and determine their responsibilities and meanings in different situations.

Whereas paradoxical intention as a technique overemphasizes the problem, dereflection is more of a diversion technique. Dereflection can be described as a self-transcendence technique, and draws on the principle of will to meaning. The idea behind dereflection is that when a person focuses too much attention on the problem it will simply exacerbate it. Therefore, with dereflection the goal is to draw their attention away from the problem. For example, if a person is too self-absorbed they would be encouraged to focus all of their attention on a loved one. This also occurs when a person with insomnia focuses so hard on sleeping that as a result they merely exacerbate the problem and lose more sleep, or when a person with compulsive disorders focus so hard on trying not to do something that they end up doing it more because they are always thinking about it. Thus the goal is not merely to make a client forget their tendencies, but to redirect them to healthier, more positive ones.

Gestalt Therapy

Gestalt therapy is a theory which is primarily credited to the work of Frederick and Laura Perls in the 1970s. The underlying concept of Gestalt therapy combines elements of humanistic, existential and phenomenological approaches. It is phenomenological in the sense that it emphasizes the relative existence of an individual, and their unique perceptions. It is humanistic and existential in the sense that there is also a large emphasis on the continually changing aspect of a person, and the becoming and developing process. This also inherently impacts humanistic qualities as it considers factors of human interactions and relationships, and the potential for individual growth.

Many people also consider Gestalt therapy to have roots in psychoanalytic theory. While Perls was likely influenced by its concepts, it deviates in a number of significant ways. For example, Freud's work considered childhood to be the most important phase in a person's life – with events and beliefs that developed at that time shaping the person's entire life. Gestalt therapy, on the other hand, defines a person much more holistically and elastically. It takes the view that people are continually changing and developing. This shifts the focus of Gestalt therapy to current situations and events, rather than the past.

Gestalt therapy also differs from psychoanalytic theory because of its emphasis on the experiences and processes of a person's interactions, rather than the content or mechanism behind them. Psychoanalytic theory, in contrast, takes a highly mechanistic view of the human condition. As a result, Gestalt therapy considers the "how" factor of individual behavior, and psychoanalytic therapies extensively consider the "why" factor in determining individual behavior.

Gestalt therapy holds a view of human nature in which individuals are considered to resist themselves and try to become things that they are not, because they perceive them to be what they "should" be becoming. Paradoxically, the theory states that this process of an individual attempting to change into something different than what they are actually causes them to stagnate, or to reach a stuck point. People change, rather, as they develop an increased understanding of who they are. If someone attempts to become something that they are not, they essentially repress a part of themselves or their character. It is the role of the therapist, therefore, to help clients understand and identify those elements which have been estranged over time.

In fact, the world Gestalt actually refers to a state of wholeness. The emphasis in Gestalt therapy on the present experience of emotions, action, and perceptions, rather than on interpreting the past or analyzing it, is in an attempt to better identify those elements which are stopping a person from being whole. Because people are naturally changing all the time, Gestalt theory asserts that they can only be understood in the context of their experiences and situations. The goal of the counselor is to help clients understand their underlying feelings and how they relate to the world around them. Ultimately this will help the client to decide how they feel about their situation, and empower them to make any desired changes to their lives.

An important concept of Gestalt therapy is that of unfinished business. In Gestalt therapy, there is considered to be a background/foreground relationship in existence among an individual's perceptions. Things which are pushed into the background, but which have not been fully resolved (and therefore continue to interfere with their ability to lead fulfilling lives) constitute unfinished business. It is important that individuals confront the emotions or situations which result in unfinished business because they obscure a person's true self and makes it more difficult to attain an increased state of self-awareness.

In addition to a high focus on a person's experiences in general, Gestalt theory also places a high emphasis specifically on relationships with others. How a person relates to both their surroundings and the people around them is referred to as contact. Contact is considered essential for personal health and growth, and the maintenance of individuality. However, it is also considered important that once a person has experienced contact, they are able to withdraw and process what they have felt and learned. For this reason, in order to be healthy, people create boundaries which serve to both connect them with the rest of the world (by creating a border which puts them in contact with others), and to separate them from the rest of the world (by allowing for independence).

If for some reason a person develops boundaries and defenses which prevent them from effectively experiencing contact, this is referred to as resistance to contact. Therapists work with clients to identify these contact-restricting barriers, in order to allow patients increased opportunities for growth. There are five basic types of resistance to contact which are acknowledged in Gestalt therapy: introjection, deflection, projection, confluence and retroflection.

Introjection occurs when individuals indiscriminately take on the characteristics that they experience through contact. In other words, while healthy individuals consider and learn from their contact experiences, and where appropriate alter what they experience to fit their own lifestyles and beliefs, individuals described by introjection merely take on the things that they experience in their entirety. This does not allow for true personal growth and can cause a sense of alienation because the individual has effectively lost their sense of identity.

Deflection is characterized by resisting a state of maintained contact. In this state, contact becomes inconsistent and unfulfilling. Rather than direct communication, individuals with this problem will generalize, deal in abstractions, and attempt to distract from a situation. Although in tense situations deflection can be a useful tool, as a continual state it blocks effective emotional interaction and results in stagnation.

Projection is most simply described as the opposite of introjection. Whereas in introjection a person indiscriminately takes on the characteristics of their environment, in projection a person applies their characteristics to their environment. Often people will project the qualities which they dislike about themselves, which prevents them from taking responsibility for their own problems. This practice is detrimental because it erodes a person's boundaries and eliminates opportunities for growth.

Confluence takes this concept of blurred boundaries and pushes it to an extreme. In this state, individuals are most concerned with blending into their environment. Essentially, this involves attempting to remove boundaries altogether. This destroys all sense of individuality and therefore makes effective contact impossible.

Finally, **retroflection** involves creating a false sense of self-sufficiency. Essentially a person will create a divide within themselves and will attempt fill their needs by either doing to themselves what they wish to do to others, or doing for themselves what they wish others would do. As with many forms of resistance to contact, retroflection can serve a useful purpose when employed properly, though it is dangerous when used in extremes. For example, when a person becomes angry it is generally more appropriate to bite their lip than to lash out at others. However, when taken to the extreme of injuring oneself in anger, retroflection becomes dangerous.

The high emphasis on experience in Gestalt therapy inherently promotes an active and lively approach to therapy. Therapists employing this method will actively seek an open relationship with their clients, with genuine concern and involvement being key factors in the therapeutic process. Gestalt therapy is largely an experimental process (not in the sense that it is untested, but rather in the sense that it involves finding ways to "test" clients and increase their own self-understanding and awareness).

The most important tool in Gestalt therapy is dialogue. Through creating a dialogue, or conversation, with the client, a counselor allows an ongoing experience and contact that can expose problems or allow the client to truly express themselves. The dialogue can be real, such as with the counselor, or it can be imagined. For example, many Gestalt therapists will have an extra chair in their office which clients can imagine a third person in. They can hold a "conversation" with this person that can help them resolve past conflicts causing them to have ongoing instability.

Phenemenological Approach

The phenomenological approach is attributed to **Edmund Husserl** in the early part of the 1900s. The focus of the phenomenological approach is a concept of self in a highly focused on first-person perspectives. An important aspect of the phenomenological approach to psychology is the complex way in which it considers experience. Experience is taken to be a relative and individual thing, and therefore knowledge and understanding are not considered to be quantifiable scientifically. The primary goal of phenomenological-based therapies is finding a way to connect with and understand a client, and to see the world from their point of view to best help them.

One important concept to understand in phenomenology is intentionality. Intentionality refers to the fact that consciousness cannot exist on its own. Rather, a person must be conscious of something (in other words, consciousness is always directed towards or through something). The implication of intentionality is that it is essentially impossible to perceive the world in an objective way. Because perceptions occur only on a basis of intentionality, each person will experience it uniquely and subjectively.

That people experience things uniquely is often referred to using the term "qualia." Qualia is essentially a description of a person's perception of a situation or object. For example, a phenomenological individual may question whether each person experiences the color red in the same way, or if they taste food the same.

The result of intentionality is that people operate in what Husserl described as a life-world. In contrast to the world of science or mathematics, the state of the life-world is highly perception based. Essentially, the life-world is the backdrop of perceptions, motivations, beliefs, and other factors that surround us and influence our consciousness and even its deepest and most basic level. The life-world is relational and dynamic. It encompasses elements such as spirituality, individuality, self-perceptions, and relationships.

Cognitive Behavioral Therapy

Cognitive-behavioral therapy is a type of psychoanalytic therapy which describes a number of different styles which focus on the ways in which cognitive and behavioral elements affect a person's health and psychological well-being. What sets cognitive-behavioral therapies apart from other therapeutic techniques is that they tend to be a much more short term and specific form of treatment.

Another common theme that runs through various cognitive-behavioral models is a collaborative relationship between counselor and client. Cognitive-behavioral therapy is highly goal motivated and specific, and places the responsibility for improvement on the client. In other words, the client is expected to take an active role both in therapy sessions and throughout the rest of their lives as well. The collaborations between counselor and client go beyond merely talking back and forth. Rather, cognitive-behavioral theories have an educational basis. Although the responsibility to change is placed on the client, the role of the counselor is to help them identify faulty thought processes, unlearn them, and learn more positive ones.

A central tool of cognitive-behavioral therapies, therefore, is assigning homework. A counselor may give their clients books or articles, or assign them specific tasks. These can have a variety of purposes, such as helping them learn more about possible cognitive failures that result in psychological and behavioral difficulties. They could also involve tasks which are useful in helping the client identify their own thought tendencies. Although the actual counseling process of cognitive-behavioral models tends towards the short term, this does not mean that it requires little effort.

A common feature of many cognitive-behavioral models is an emphasis on cognitive functions as the motivations behind actions. In fact, the most important premises are that psychological problems are a result of faulty cognitive processes, and that changing cognitive processes will result in improved behaviors. As a result of this belief, the inductive method, or patients considering their own thoughts, is an important element of cognitive-behavioral therapy. The Socratic method is also quite often used.

Cognitive-behavioral therapy is used in treating phobias, addictions, anxiety, and depression among other problems. It does not even really have to be applied to individuals with mental health problems, but can be useful for people who simply have a high-stress life as well. The most well-known cognitive-behavioral therapy styles are cognitive therapy and rational emotive behavioral therapy.

Cognitive therapy is a theory which was developed by psychiatrist Aaron T. Beck, and it falls under the larger branch of cognitive-behavioral therapies. Cognitive therapy most directly relates to issues of depression, but can be extended to other situations too. For example, Beck's theories have been applied to academic difficulties and difficulties in work environments. Beck's theory is that depression is caused by the natural tendency of individuals to have a negative pattern of thought. In other words, people who are depressed have a negative bias in their view of the world which serves to reinforce their depression. Because the theory asserts that thoughts are what eventually prompt actions and further thoughts, all that is necessary is to train individuals to have a more positive thought process.

Cognitive therapy has three basic theoretical assertions associated with it. First, a client can understand their internal thought processes through introspection. In other words, it is important that clients become aware of the "automatic thoughts" which result in various situations. Because these automatic thoughts are going to be reflective of the client's overall disposition, they will have a large effect on the client's actions.

The second principle regards the fact that client's thought processes and beliefs have personal meanings. In other words, there is a specific reason or underlying belief behind the client's negative thought process which is relevant to them. For example, two clients may both have inferiority problems, but they may have different underlying thought processes which cause the problem. For example, for one it may stem from a belief that they have to be the best to be worth anything, whereas for the other it may be a result of over generalizing and considering one mistake to be their defining characteristic.

The third principle, which logically follows from the first two, is that the client can discover the meanings behind their thought processes (i.e., they don't need to be told what they are). Considering these three principles as a whole, the resulting structure of cognitive-behavioral therapy is to encourage clients to become more aware of their thought process, such as by writing down or in some way tracking their thoughts, and then for the counselor and client to collaborate in determining the possible faulty thought processes behind these thought patterns. From here, a client can work to determine the motivations behind these processes, and alter their mindset to a more productive and useful one.

Cognitive therapy identifies many different types of faulty thought processes which lead to depression. All-or-nothing thinking is the idea that there can be no middle ground. For example, an individual may convince themselves that they "always" do the wrong thing, that they will "never" understand, or that they "always" do the "worst." Another faulty thought process is referred to as overgeneralization, which is when a person takes a single instance and assumes that it is always that way. This sort of thinking is closely tied to all-or-nothing thought.

Mental filter is another term describing a faulty thought process in cognitive theory which can lead to depression. Mental filter is a tendency to only see the negative aspect of a situation, or to essentially filter out any positives. Mental filter can also refer to an individual seeing only the information that confirms their point of view, and ignoring everything else. This is similar to disqualifying the positive, which describes situations in which a person treats positive situations as though they are less relevant that the negative ones, or believes that they don't really count.

Other thought processes which cognitive therapy attempts to isolate and change are personalization, or blaming oneself for situations that can't be controlled; magnification, or paying close attention to negative situations; jumping to conclusions, or automatically believing the worst about a situation; and should statements, or focusing on how a situation "should be" rather than how it is. It is the goal of cognitive therapy to help individuals identify these thought patterns and to change them to have a more hopeful and positive process of thought, leading to a happier life.

Rational Emotive Behavior Therapy

The second important cognitive-behavioral therapy, Rational Emotive Behavior Therapy (REBT) was developed by Albert Ellis in the 1950s. Ellis believed that all people are born with the capability of both rational and irrational thought. Based on this, individuals create perceptions or beliefs which then influence their emotions and actions. In other words, individuals contribute to their own happiness or anger or any other emotion.

This consideration is fairly unique in that it asserts that people have an inherent potential to move towards happiness, fulfillment and positive relationships; however, it also asserts that they equally have an inherent potential to move towards self-destructive and negative behaviors. The result of this is that REBT considers people to naturally learn and develop both positive and negative characteristics and behaviors. The emphasis becomes to help individuals accept themselves and their flaws, while also encouraging them to consciously move towards more beneficial tendencies.

REBT is often modeled with the A-B-C theory, in which "A" is a situation, "B" is a person's belief about that situation, and "C" is their emotional response to that situations. For example, if the situation ("A") is that a person is fired, and they believe ("B") that it was unjustified, it would likely result in the individual feeling angry ("C"). This sets up a pattern which human behavior can be modeled after. Using this model it can be easily seen that a different belief about the situation, such as if the individual instead believed that getting fired was their own fault (resulting in a new step "B"), the result would be a completely different outcome. Instead of feeling angry, they would feel either ashamed or guilty or disappointed in themselves as the case may be. Hence the two different beliefs about the situation result in completely opposite resulting feelings and behaviors. For this reason, the theory asserts that beliefs cause responses, not situations.

Inherent in this model is the implication that the three human aspects of thought, action, and belief are highly interrelated and connected. According to Ellis, rarely can any single aspect be experienced purely. For example, most emotion will arise from a certain thought or thought process. Similarly these emotions and thoughts can be directly linked to actions. This is what makes the REBT model a cognitive-behavioral theory.

Based on this model, emotional disturbances are caused by an individual's repetition of unhealthy beliefs over time. For example, if a person believes that they are a failure, that everything is their fault, that they have been unjustly treated, that they have to have things their way, or any other of the many possible negative beliefs possible, it will result in consistently detrimental reactions. Therefore, a person's belief systems are self-perpetuating – whether for the better or the worse in the long run.

Ellis identified three basic thought processes (which people can develop and adapt in any number of variations based on their personal situations) which are irrational and unhealthy in the long run. He referred to these three belief systems as the "three basic musts." The first of the basic musts is the belief that to be worth anything, you must be successful and obtain the approval of others. By adhering to this belief, a person essentially places their own happiness in the hands of others. This most often leads to anxiety, depression, guilt, and self-esteem issues.

The second of the basic musts is the belief that if people don't treat us kindly and considerately (or exactly how we wish them to treat us), then they are inherently bad people and deserve punishment. This and related beliefs are inflexible, which makes them rather unrealistic. It is characterized by a refusal to acknowledge that people make mistakes, and is unforgiving. This second belief often leads to anger issues, passive-aggressive behavior, an inability to accept criticism, and excessive conflict with others.

The third of the basic musts is essentially the belief that life should be easy. For example, it could be manifested in a person's belief that they should always be able to get what they want or work for. It could also manifest through an inability to accept inconvenient or uncomfortable situations, or a person's belief that they are not able to cope with trials. These thought processes often result in self-pitying, depression, frustration or procrastination.

In response to the natural A-B-C model which Ellis observed, he developed additional steps to the model to allow individuals to remedy their thought processes and eventually their life outlooks. In order for it to be effective, however, first requires that individuals acknowledge that the situations that they are in are only a small factor in their emotions and responses in different situations. Far more important are their beliefs. Once this has been acknowledged, individuals must begin seeking to understand how and why they have developed, and continue to develop, self-defeating thought processes. According to Ellis, behaviors and processes learned in the past will continue to manifest and need to be identified if they are to be addressed. The most important factor in making REBT successful, however, is that the client works continuously to attempt to modify and improve their thoughts. Merely recognizing faulty attitudes will not cause them to change.

To bring about a change, Ellis argued the importance of a disputation phase, described as step "D." This phase is termed the disputing phase because that is what its purpose is – for an individual to dispute their own beliefs. The disputation step is further broken down into three stages: detecting, debating and discriminating. Detecting refers to simply identifying the process and its origin. This is following by debating, through which a client works to consider their belief from an objective and empirical standpoint to determine whether it is logical or irrational. Discrimination refers to an ability to in fact determine which beliefs are irrational and must be replaced.

Once an irrational belief has been determined through disputation, a client will be at step E. Ellis referred to this as the "effect." Step E is the resulting philosophy that emerges when a client determines that their current belief is wrong. Step E is basically a more practical and effective philosophy held by the individual. Positive and healthy thoughts replace the old, unhealthy ones. This leads to F – a new set of feelings. It is important that individuals are constantly cycling through the D – E – F part of the cycle to ensure that new attitudes do not develop that are detrimental.

The goal of a counselor in REBT is, therefore, to help patients identify situations in which it is their incorrect beliefs which are the problem. For example, if a student failed an important exam, they would likely feel that failing the exam was making them feel frustrated and depressed. However, a therapist may identify that it is the student's resulting belief that they are useless and worthless that is the problem, and help them to overcome those feelings. Ellis emphasized that people should separate their tendency to judge and rate their actions from their beliefs about themselves, arguing that this was often the cause of dysfunctional thought processes. He believed that individuals should learn to accept themselves unconditionally.

The next major branch of therapy to consider is behavioral therapy. Behavior therapy is a type of therapy which focuses on helping clients improve their moods and attitudes through altering their actions. Because of this it can also be referred to as behavior modification therapy. The theory of behavior therapy was developed primarily by B. F. Skinner, and is a sharp departure from the psychoanalytic methods of the time. Skinner believed that because actions and environments were the only things that could be directly observed; they are the only things which can be assumed to affect a person (he therefore rejected the relevance of a soul). Skinner's greatest contribution to psychology was the development of the operant conditioning model.

The first scientific experiment of **classical conditioning** was done by a Russian scientist named Ivan Pavlov. In Pavlov's famous dog experiment, he would ring a bell and then feed the dogs. Initially, the dogs would salivate when given food. Over time, the dogs began to salivate at the sound of the bell. Classical conditioning describes a link between a stimulus and a response in which a person or animal associates or substitutes a neutral stimulus, such as the bell, with the actual stimulus, the food. Many reflexive reactions, such as a person covering their eyes when something flies in front of their face, or salivating at the smell of their favorite food, can be explained through classical conditioning.

A more modern application of **classical conditioning** is the idea of systematic desensitization. **Systematic desensitization** is a process which uses the principles of classical conditioning as a treatment for anxiety disorders and phobias. The process of systematic desensitization involves an individual imagining themselves in stressful or frightening situations, and teaching themselves to respond calmly. As the person becomes more comfortable with their fears, they can transfer from imagined situations to actual situations, and because of the process of classical conditioning they will respond in the same, calm manner. For example, if a person has a fear of heights they may imagine themselves on tall buildings or bridges. Then, when they actually encounter these situations they will have become desensitized to the fear.

In contrast to classical conditioning, **B. F. Skinner** developed a conditioning model referred to as operant conditioning. Operant conditioning is a type of conditioning in which a person associates an action with a consequence. The main difference between operant conditioning and classical conditioning is that classical conditioning works more to explain reflexive or unconscious reactions, whereas operant conditioning works to explain elective actions and reactions. For example, a student will wish to do well in school because it brings the consequence of good grades and parental approval. Studies have shown that even infants can be taught certain behaviors using operant conditioning.

In either form, conditioning depends upon reinforcers as a method of learning. A reinforcer is anything which makes a behavior more likely to reoccur. Reinforcers can be positive or negative. A positive reinforcer is when something pleasant is used to make a behavior more likely. Parents paying their children for good grades or a person giving their pet a treat for doing a trick are both examples of positive reinforcers. A negative reinforcer is when something unpleasant is removed from a situation. For example, if a student studies more, they are less anxious. The anxiety is an unpleasant feeling which is removed as a result of studying, and therefore studying is a form of negative reinforcement. Conditioning can also occur using punishments, which instead of making a behavior more likely to reoccur, attempt to make it less likely to reoccur. Like reinforcers, punishments can be both positive and negative.

In addition to being positive and negative, reinforcers can also be described as extrinsic or intrinsic.

An **extrinsic reinforcer** is something physical (tangible), or from the environment. Payment for work, a treat for doing well, and earning a prize for winning a game are all extrinsic reinforcers. An intrinsic reinforcer, on the other hand, is something which comes from within the individual, or in other words, something emotional. Self-satisfaction or the happiness which comes from praise are intrinsic reinforcers. The values of extrinsic and intrinsic reinforcers are different for everyone.

Systems Therapy

Systems theory is a broad category which has been applied to many different types of therapy. Systems therapy is a practice of moving problems from an individual or singular basis, to placing them in the context of a whole; i.e., a system. At its foundation, systems therapy resists the notion that individuals can be understood by exhaustively studying the minute details or factors at work within them (as do most theories; e.g., Freud focused on the unconscious mind and childhood experiences). This branch of therapy further resists the notion that an individual can be understood even in the context of studying the many factors within them. Rather, people are considered with the larger perspective of the social structures and organizations around them.

The original application of systems theory was in the field of biology, where its founder argued that science should be considered both in terms of breaking things down to their basic parts and in terms of their interrelatedness. For example, although to understand an atom it is necessary to study its components (protons, neutrons, and electrons), simply studying these units extensively will not yield an understanding of the atom as a whole. Taken from this point of view, systems therapy as it applies to counseling is essentially a theory of interconnectedness of individuals and problems, and it advocates a community-minded perspective.

Systems therapy marks a large departure from the more traditional analytic approach. It seeks to neither determine or catalog the influences that past events have in a person's life, nor to diagnose individuals in terms of their current behavior. Rather, the central purpose of systems therapy is to analyze the relationships of individuals in a system, and urge more productive and healthy relational patterns.

One of the most common applications of systems therapy is to family therapy (for this reason it is also referred to as family systems therapy). The primary focus of family therapy is to improve relations within a family. The primary objective of the therapist in family therapy is to understand the interactions that occur between people, rather than analyzing the actions or conflicts within a specific individual. Family therapists also tend to be less focused on specific or individual causes of conflicts, and more interested in the bigger picture of how the individuals react to each other. A family systems therapist may consider transgenerational issues, or try to determine how family interactions are resulting in a client's difficulties.

Systems therapy has also been broadened in its application to refer to essentially any situation in which people are required to act in a cohesive unit. For example, in businesses where individuals find themselves working in close contact with others on a regular basis, or sports teams which must learn to function in a highly organized manner. Other fields of interest in systemic theory may include politics, education, or social work. In each case there is a large focus on the interactions between individuals, and the organizational structure of the unit.

Systems therapy places a large emphasis on the maintenance of homeostasis in an environment. In other words, it focuses on the creation of a balance among individuals within the system. However, because systems can often involve groups of many very different individuals, relationships tend to be dynamic and constantly shifting. This factor brings about the concept of dynamic equilibrium. Dynamic equilibrium refers to a state in which things are constantly changing, and yet the overall balance of the system is maintained. Communication is one of the most important elements of systems therapy.

Eclectic Theory

The next major branch of therapy to be considered is eclectic theory. In considering the many other fields of therapy which have been discussed, it can be seen that in many cases the theories have a tendency to overlap and modify one another. For example, cognitive-behavioral therapies share a number of similarities with behavioral therapies. As another example, the classification of therapies such as Gestalt therapy becomes different because it was influenced by and displays characteristics of so many different branches – including humanistic, existential, psychoanalytic, and phenomenological. Although the many different branches do have their characteristics which make them distinct from others, in practice they can share many characteristics. As a result, the eclectic practice developed.

Eclecticism essentially describes a practice of considering multiple theories in the treatment of a patient. Counseling is a very unique field filled with hundreds of thousands of different people with different problems and different possible solutions. Although historically many counselors and psychologists would tend to pick one type of counseling theory and stick with it in all situations, the more common practice has become to use multiple different techniques as specific situations and problems may demand.

An eclectic therapist must therefore have a very broad knowledge base which encompasses a number of different therapies. The main benefit of this style is that it allows a large amount of flexibility in treatment, so that if a client's situation changes, or if a particular strategy proves too difficult or incompatible with their personality, the counselor can adapt to better help them. Also, often different theories will be most applicable to certain situations. For example, while cognitive-behavioral models tend to address problems of depression, other models consider addictions and phobias. An eclectic counselor can therefore help patients across a number of different problem bases.

This dynamic aspect of eclectic therapy requires that a counselor and patient have a strong relationship and communicate effectively. The counselor should have the ability to accurately identify the specific problems which the patient is struggling with and be able to competently determine what approach to take to best help them.

Eclectic therapy is primarily an experience-based practice. In other words, the therapist will make determinations and take action based on what they have seen used successfully in the past. Often this becomes a criticism of eclectic practice because as a result it does not need have any specified framework.

It is also important to understand, however, that eclectic therapy does not require that a counselor merely consider various types of therapies, but involves an integration of their principles in treatment. In other words, it does not describe a counselor simply jumping randomly from a psychodynamic form of treatment to one based on Ellis's REBT theory to a sort of phenomenological approach. Rather, the counselor would more likely begin with a discussion through which they attempt to identify the relevance of psychodynamic and cognitive factors. They may then give patients tasks and assignments to complete which they believe will help them to progress, thereby integrating the homework aspect of cognitive-behavioral methods with psychodynamic therapy.

Holistic Therapy

The term holistic therapy is used to describe any sort of treatment or counseling which takes a holistic or comprehensive approach to healing. Holistic therapy is also often called alternative therapy because it incorporates methods other than the traditional medication or counseling approach. This is what makes holistic therapy so unique.

While the majority of the techniques discussed thus far have dealt primarily with cognitive functions and their impacts on behavior (and in some cases vice versa), holistic therapy considers the overall vitality and well-being of the client.

The idea behind holistic therapy is that for a person to be truly healthy they must be strong and confident emotionally, physically, spiritually and mentally. Holistic therapies may be a combination of many other types of therapies or something entirely unique. The number of treatments which can be and are used in holistic therapies is extremely diverse. A factor which is inherently taken into consideration with holistic therapy is that often different areas and treatments can overlap. For example, a person who is working through anger management issues, which would be considered an emotional problem, may be simultaneously improving their health, a physical factor, by having a lower average blood pressure.

From the physical perspective there are many different angles which a person can consider. For example, a person's literal day-to-day health practices may be considered. Holistic therapy may consider factors such as the client's nutrition, and prescribe more balanced and healthy eating habits. Herbal and other remedies are also a consideration of holistic therapy. When considering herbal remedies however, it is often wise to do thorough research to determine the source of the remedy. If it is based in folk lore or rumor, it may not have any merit as a treatment, and may even prove to be dangerous if used unwisely. However, many herbs have been scientifically studied and shown to yield natural positive health effects. Because of this it is important to be well informed and up to date about such issues before engaging in holistic treatments.

The physical aspect can also be considered as it relates to a client's exercise and wellness habits. From an exercise perspective, yoga, Pilates, or any regular exercise regimen may be advised. Exercise naturally releases endorphins, resulting in sensations of happiness and relaxation. It is also an effective weight-loss technique and can therefore help the patient to feel more accomplished and positive about themselves.

Where a client's mental health is concerned is where the various other forms of therapy are integrated. Due to its diverse nature, holistic therapy tends to have a more eclectic approach. Psychotherapy, cognitive-behavioral, humanistic, and really any other therapeutic approach may be employed as will be suit the needs of the client. It is important to understand that simply because holistic therapy employs many different methods in treatment, doesn't mean that it discounts the more traditional approaches of therapy and medication. Rather, it emphasizes that these treatments be added to with additional treatments aimed at increasing the client's health in a well-rounded manner.

Emotional therapy involves any actions which are taken to better understand and improve the emotional state of a client. Patients undergoing major life changes may need a specific focus on the emotional difficulties that they cause. For example, the death of a spouse or other significant individual, entering the "empty nest" stage of life, divorce, marriage, or other emotionally taxing events. Emotional issues are often deeply connected with all of the other areas of holistic therapy.

One form of treatment specifically directed towards a client's emotional state is art therapy, which allows a visual expression of emotion, and often can result in a therapeutic release of tension in the client. Another well-known emotional therapy is Emotional Freedom Technique (referred to as EFT) which is somewhat similar to acupuncture, and has the goal of releasing (in other words freeing) negative emotional buildup in the body. In some cases, simple practices such as decluttering living environments or allowing for personal relaxation time can result in a greatly improved overall emotional state.

One of the most common emotional issues that needs to be addressed is the problem of stress and anxiety. Treatments for stress can range from the simple, such as engaging in a hobby, taking time off from work, or counting to ten, to the more involved. For example, acupuncture, massage therapy, feng shui, and meditation can all be used to relieve stress and create a more productive and emotionally stimulating environment.

Spiritual Health

Spiritual health is also an important aspect in holistic therapy. One way to approach the spiritual element of holistic therapy is by consider the client's religious involvement and beliefs. A client's religious views can be a useful tool in their recovery process. Religious groups can offer a strong foundation of support for clients. Faith can be a source of psychological stability, and in many cases church groups can offer a social aspect which creates a sense of community and inclusion. In terms of incorporating religious views into therapy, however, views are mixed. This is because although for some patients religion is a positive life influence, for others it may be a source of distress or difficulty. Because every situation is different it is important that counselor consider the details of each case to decide what the appropriate action is.

Also, religious beliefs are not the only consideration regarding spiritual well-being. While religious views can be an important part of spiritual health, it also applies to a general sense of heightened awareness. For example, through meditation, introspection, or other methods, individuals can gain a deepened understanding of themselves and the world around them. This is increased awareness and openness indicates spiritual well-being.

Feminist Therapy

Another interesting type of multicultural therapy involves feminist therapy. While feminist therapy may not be a form of multicultural therapy in the strictest sense, it is often considered along with multicultural therapies because of its clear cultural implications. In fact, feminist therapy strives to be independent of culture. Rather, it is intended to span cultural differences and become universally applicable and beneficial women in any cultural situation. As follows from the name, feminist therapy is primarily geared towards understanding the effects of gender on a person's life, and opening up as many opportunities as possible for a client. Feminist therapists should consider tactics which will facilitate this empowerment, such as increased education, values, and participation in support groups.

The origins of feminist therapy can be traced back to the feminist movement in the 1960s. It was during this time that female therapists and women in general, began to speak out against traditional therapeutic models. Their argument was that the theories were inadequate in dealing with the situations of women because they were developed and practiced from a male dominated perspective. Women argued that this resulted in a system which was actually more psychologically damaging for many women than it was helpful.

For example, traditional psychoanalytic models view anxiety and depression (two of the most common psychological difficulties faced by women) as a product of internal conflicts and pressures. This places responsibility for the problem within the woman, rather than acknowledging unrealistic social pressures which she may be subject to. Because women tend to focus on relationships and responsibilities to others, often the cause of anxiety can be traced external factors which are trivialized in psychoanalysis. As a result, feminist therapy focuses on empowering women and teaching clients to recognize the forces in their lives which may constrain or demean them.

There are essentially four different approaches to feminist therapy: liberal, cultural, social, and radical feminism. A therapist may employ different tactics and methods based on which specific model they ascribe to. While each of the approaches is focused on sources of oppression and how to induce change, each takes a unique perspective. Liberal feminist theory is highly focused on empowerment. It strives to create open and bias-free environments in which women can overcome the limitations inherent in their socialization patterns.

The cultural feminist model takes an essentially opposite position to liberal feminism. Whereas liberal feminism focuses on uplifting the situation of women, and on eliminating barriers and creating equality, cultural feminism focuses on increasing the value of existing cultural distinctions. Cultural feminists believe that society has traditionally devalued the role women as nurturers and homemakers, and that bringing value to these roles is how women can become empowered. The goal of this therapy, then, is to embed female values (cooperation, relationships, nurturing, intuition, etc.) into culture.

Radical feminist theory places an emphasis on the role of patriarchy in subjugating women. In other words, radical feminists believe that society has created a pattern of male dominance that is overtly suppressive to women in all areas of life (including housework, employment, intimacy, and parenting). Because the goal of radical feminism is to elevate women through eliminating this inherent patriarchy, it is typically considered the most aggressive approach to feminism; however, this is not necessarily the case. Although some of its supporters do take on violent or hostile dispositions, a majority of its supporters manifest their beliefs by acting against rape, domestic violence, and sexual harassment.

A common misconception about radical feminist therapy is the role of blame. Radical feminist therapy is not, in fact, centered on blaming men for suppression of women. Nor does it encourage an inherent hatred of men. Rather, the main goal of feminist therapy is to achieve recognition that the current social structure is suppressive to women. Once this is recognized, it is then possible to begin altering the social structure to allow for the empowerment of women.

The final perspective is socialist feminism. Socialist feminism takes by far the broadest perspective of any of the four perspectives. Whereas radical feminism views female suppression as the primary form of suppression in society (or the one which all others are based off of), socialist feminism considers oppression in context of the many forms in which it exists in society. The goal of socialist feminism is society reform targeting multiple forms of oppression, including problems which arise as a result of race, socio-economic status, culture, image, and gender. Essentially, if a person is a poor, female, African American, then they are three times worse off than a rich, white, male individual. Therefore, the avenue through which true equality can be created is by eliminating all forms of oppression within society.

In considering the techniques of feminist therapy, a variety of approaches can be taken based on the perspectives of the specific counselor and client. However, there are certain characteristics and tactics which are important in any case. One of the most important qualities for a counselor to exhibit is an egalitarian belief system, or a strong belief in equality. This means that the counselor needs to be aware of the roles that the client occupies in their lives. However, at least as equally important is attention to the relationship which exists between the counselor and client. In feminist therapy it is important that the counselor does not place themselves above the client, such as by creating the impression aloofness or expertise. They should be open in their discussion with clients in order to facilitate openness in return.

Gender-role analysis is a common practice of feminist therapy. This involves discussing the effects of gender stereotypes on the client, and attempting to help them see the positive and negative effects with these stereotypes have had. Considering these expectations is meant to empower clients by allowing them to identify the societal problems which may cause them psychological distress. If expectations are identified with negative impacts, it becomes possible to intervene and work with the client to change their perceptions of themselves and their role.

Another common practice is power analysis and intervention. This technique is similar to gender role analysis, but it encourages women to analyze the power dynamic that exists in their social interactions. They should consider both the power that others influence over them, and the situations in which they influence power over others. This can help clients see the areas in which they do have strength, and appreciate themselves for their accomplishments.

Reframing and relabeling are also important techniques in feminist therapy. Reframing is the process of discovering the external factors which lead to depression, anxiety, or other feelings of inadequacy. For example, a woman would be encouraged to consider the ways that media and advertisements influence her self-concept, rather than considering herself to be deficient or failing in some way. Hence she changes her frame of references (or reframes) in how she perceives herself. Relabeling involves a process of changes the labels which a person has attached to themselves, often as a result of reframing.

Feminist therapy also involves a practice of considering behavioral, emotional, and physical factors in context. For example, an important characteristic of feminist therapy is a consideration of life-span. Whereas many traditional therapies consider specific times during an individual's life to be of particular importance (e.g., Freud focused on childhood, Jung on mid-life, and Perls on immediate situations), feminist therapy considers the evolution of a woman (or man) and her place in society. There is a view of interconnectedness when considering the social, political, and personal aspects of an individual.

Finally, feminist therapy works to alter understandings and beliefs about what "mental illness" is. Traditional therapeutic practices consider anxiety and depression as effects entirely of internal processes. In feminist therapy, external influences and environments are considered as important as psychological factors in creating problems. Rather than classifying clients and creating a mentality of illness and distress, feminist therapy works to connect an impression of resistance and attributes strength to those involved in therapy. Counselors in feminist therapy should work to create an accepting, egalitarian atmosphere to best help and empower clients.

 Religion in Therapy

In addition to the considerations of gender and race or ethnicity in therapy, religion is also an important cultural implication that counselors should be able to handle. The vast majority of people in the United States identify themselves with some form of organized religion. In an even broader sense, every individual is affected by their own beliefs regarding spirituality. Although spirituality and religion are often considered to be distinct terms, in many cases they may be interchangeable. Religion is essentially an organized belief system. The term religion is applied to the many different churches to which a person can ascribe (e.g., Catholicism, Protestantism, Hinduism, Buddhism, etc.). It includes the institutional setting of worship, interactions with other members, and dogmas or frameworks of morality. Religions teach moral guidelines and value systems by which individuals should live their lives.

Spirituality has a much looser definition, and because of this many people consider it to be a more useful consideration in a counseling setting. Spirituality is essentially an individual's process of self-expression. It encompasses their personal beliefs about intrinsic values and meanings in life. Although spirituality is often deeply intertwined with religious beliefs, this does not need to be the case. An individual can have a concept of spirituality that is theistic, agnostic, or anywhere in between. Spirituality is completely defined by an individual's own goals, and by their own sense of meaning and purpose.

When considering either spirituality or religion it is important for counselors to adequately address the effects that they have in the lives of clients. Both spirituality and religion influence the way that people perceive themselves, and affect many important decisions such as who and when to marry, how to interact with and treat others, political beliefs, and what things are or aren't ethical. Religion can be a useful tool in counseling because it can be a source of support and community for individuals suffering with addictions or other difficulties. It can also be an important influence in creating bonds between individuals in family, group, or marriage counseling. In addition, considering the role of spirituality in a person's life can help them identify areas where their own beliefs are in conflict with societal pressures, and alter their lifestyle as necessary to eliminate it as a source of stress and anxiety.

The wide-ranging application of religion and spirituality in counseling makes it important that counselors be sensitive to religious and spiritual issues as they may affect their clients. Just as counselors should make themselves aware of the cultural background and life situation of their clients, they should understand their views on spirituality. Ignoring these concerns would effectively eliminate an entire aspect of a client which could be essential in effectively counseling them. It is also important for counselors to consider the ways in which their own beliefs may be influencing the counseling relationship. One of the difficulties which can arise for counselors is when they hold differing spiritual or religious views than their clients.

In cases where the counselor and client share religious views it can be an avenue for the counselor to create a strong, positive relationship with the client. The shared beliefs can create a basis from which to consider the client's health, and allow the counselor a framework from which to advise clients. However, if a counselor's views differ from those of their client they should be careful not to make the client feel displaced or uncomfortable. Rather, the counselor should be open and considerate with the client. In fact, the ACA Code of Ethics requires that counselors do not discriminate against clients on a basis of their religious beliefs. Counselors should always remember that it is not the goal of counseling to change a client's views, or to enforce a particular set of values. When clients are experiencing a change or conflict in religious views the counselor should be encouraging in their exploration of different views, and help them try to understand the motivations behind their changing opinions.

Discrimination

In addition to these many cultural and socioeconomic considerations in counseling, discrimination is another major issue which is often confronted in counseling situations. While some of the most prevalent forms of discrimination involve cultural considerations which have already been discussed (race, nationality, ethnicity, and gender), many additional forms of discrimination also exist. These include factors such as disability, age, sexual orientation, AIDS, and managed care. Each of these factors creates an opportunity for discrimination to occur both in an individual's personal life, and within the counseling framework. As a result counselors need to both be aware both of the social implications of these issues, and be constantly striving to eliminate forms of discrimination within their practice.

One of the primary laws regarding discrimination and equality is the Civil Rights Act. According to the Act, a person may not be discriminated against based on their race, color, religion, gender or nationality. Additional laws such as the ADA and various executive orders extend protections to individuals in areas of concern including disabilities, sexual orientations, and AIDS. The applications of the law are fairly straightforward, namely, all individuals must be treated with equality, dignity, and respect regardless of their social, cultural, or economic circumstances.

The Americans with Disabilities Act (ADA) is designed to ensure that people with disabilities receive the same opportunities as people without disabilities. The act applies to all government agencies and labor unions. The law also extends to private employers with more than 15 employees. The provisions of the ADA can be applied both to the treatment of disabled individuals, and the physical structure of the office or building. As a result of the ADA, office spaces should be designed to be accessible to disabled clients. For example, it may be required that a ramp is installed which leads to the front doors to ensure that all clients can access the building. It also extends to considerations such as adequate hall width and navigation space in bathrooms and offices. Counselors are required to make reasonable accommodations for clients with disabilities, such as providing interpreters for clients who use sign language and providing access to Braille materials or materials on tape.

A number of concerns arise when considering techniques to be used in counseling individuals with disabilities. One of the first matters that a counselor should address when working with disabled clients is a thorough assessment of their own preexisting perceptions of the individual or of a disability in general. A counselor cannot refuse to work with a client on a basis of their disability. (Of course, cases in which a client has a specific need which a counselor is not qualified to address are a different matter.) Some common responses to disability range from being overly protective or sympathetic on the one end of the spectrum to being cold, awkward, or unsure of how to respond on the other. In either case the best antidote is for the counselor to become more informed about the causes and implications of the disability. Better education regarding the needs relating to disabilities will allow a more genuine and effective counseling relationship to develop.

Learning more about the needs of disabled individuals includes gaining a better understanding about the historical treatment of disabled individuals, and how it affects their status today. Prior to the ADA, individuals with disabilities were commonly segregated and isolated from the rest of the population. It is only in more recent times that attempts have been made to empower and integrate individuals with disabilities. As a result, disabled clients may have difficulty dealing with perceptions of isolation or separation from other individuals. They may be easily frustrated or discouraged. For clients with such difficulties, it is important to emphasize the many organizations which exist to help, and the many opportunities for growth which are available to them.

Counselors should also make an effort to consider both the client's disability and external factors which are not related to the disability when working with disabled clients. Finding a balance between considering a disabled client holistically (and not overemphasizing their disability) and considering the unique factors associated with a client's disability is a difficult process. For example, it would be ineffective for a counselor to dismiss a client's depression as a by-product of their disability when the depression was truly a result of a strained relationship with a family member. However, it would also be problematic if a counselor, by attempting to avoid the issue of disability, attributed a client's depression to a strained relationship when it was truly a result of frustrations caused by their disability. In either case, the counselor would go down the wrong path in counseling the client and could actually make the problem worse with time.

A simple way to avoid this mistake is for counselors to be clear with clients. They can engage in open discussion, such as inquiring into the nature, extent, and effects of the disability. They can even ask if the client considers their disability to be a part of the problem. Based on the client's response the counselor can then either consider other possible sources of problems, or begin working to empower the client and help them deal more effectively with their disability. The proper response will depend on the client's specific perspective of their disability. Three basic models exist relating to how an individual views their disability. These models can also be applied to how people in general consider disabilities. The three models are the moral model, the medical model, and the minority model.

The moral model is much more characteristic of historical perceptions, but in some cultures it has extended into the current day. This is the view that disability emerges as a result of moral failings of either parents or the affected individual. It results in shame or embarrassment manifested in both the client and their family. This model is often tied to a certain religious or spiritual view, so finding proper religious support for the individual or their family could be a necessary step. Efforts should also be made to lift the client out of their negative perceptions and empower them by emphasizing the qualities and talents which they possess.

The medical model is a somewhat more common perception in modern times. This perception has a high focus on the medical causes and implication of the disability. The problem with this model of perception is that it emphasizes the inadequacies that the disability causes. Under this model, disabilities become a deficiency or loss to the individual which separate them from the norm. While there is no moral fault or embarrassment associated with this model, it still creates an inherent medical fault for the disability. For clients with this perception of their disability, one way to improve their self-perceptions could be to introduce technological innovations which enable them to feel like they "fit in" to the greatest extent possible. Emphasizing the ways that disability makes an individual unique is also appropriate.

The final model, the minority model, is radically different from either of the two models because it represents a shift from inward to outward blame. With this model, blame is placed on society for not creating an environment in which the individual can function normally. Essentially it is the view that the problem is not the individual's disability, but that society has not conformed to a standard which accommodates it. The most appropriate response to this model is to emphasize a pattern of self-empowerment and advocacy. The individual should be encouraged to work to improve their situations to the extent that they can, and see the opportunities that they have to influence the world around them.

In addition to the counselor's perceptions and the client's perceptions, it can also be useful to consider the impact that the client's family has on their life. Often for individuals with disabilities the family is the most important structure in their life. Families provide the majority of care and support for clients. Considering the strength of the family relationship, the family's treatment of the disability, or the extent to which the family may perpetuate the disability can provide useful insights in the counseling process.

 AIDS

Acquired Immune Deficiency Syndrome (AIDS) is one disease which deserves particular mention. AIDS has come to be classified as a disability. As a result, the protections of the ADA extent to clients with AIDS, and many of the guidelines for counseling individuals with AIDS correspond to those for dealing with other disabilities. For example, counselors may not refuse to work with an individual on a basis of their diagnosis. It is also important that counselors are aware of the specific needs and problems which affect individuals with AIDS.

AIDS affects millions of people across all age groups within the United States, and is a leading cause of death in individuals between the ages 22-44. Although some AIDS patients may live for a few years, most die within 18 months of diagnosis. The responses of patients to their diagnosis may range from grief, emptiness, and loneliness, to resentment, blame, and anger. Counselors need to be prepared to help fulfill two different roles: education and support.

In terms of education, a client may have questions regarding what to expect from their illness. Counselors can be must useful to their clients by being informed about the most recent studies and information about AIDS. There is still much that is not understood about the disease, and this can be a source of anxiety. Another educational role of counselors is in helping to raise awareness about AIDS, and counseling clients in safe practices (this is especially relevant for school counselors, but may be applicable in other settings). Counselors can also be helpful to clients by directing them towards resources such as support groups.

This leads to the supporting role of counselors. The support role of counselors in dealing with AIDS patients is in creating an open, sympathetic, and reassuring environment. As a result of rampant misconceptions about the disease, individuals affected by AIDS often feel isolated and ostracized by those around them. As a result, one of the primary roles of a counselor regarding clients with AIDS is to act as a source of hope and comfort. Even if the individual does not face discrimination from those around them they may feel fear, uncertainty, and grief as a result of their prognosis. Again, in such cases counselors can provide hope and support for their clients.

Another situation which counselors must be comfortable addressing is discrimination on a basis of sexual orientation. Laws do exist which prevent federal programs and employees from discriminating on a basis of sexual orientation. However, as yet no laws exist regarding the practice of private business or individuals. As a result, if a counselor feels uncomfortable or unqualified to work with a client with concerns regarding sexual orientation, they may simply refer them to another counselor. Of course, they should be delicate in handling the matter.

Counselors who do address matters of sexual orientation should feel comfortable discussing the matter with their clients. In all areas of counseling not specific to sexual orientation, clients should be treated exactly like any other client. The primary issue of concern specific to gay or lesbian clients is the matter of sexual identity. Counselors should be supportive of clients, and help them in working through concerns or questions that they may have about their sexual identity. The first step in counseling gay and lesbian clients is determining their level of acceptance. Clients with low levels of acceptance of their feelings will often feel distress, anxiety, or confusion about them. Clients with more midrange levels of acceptance will often exhibit a more proactive pride or outward support for their orientation in an attempt to assure themselves and reinforce their feelings. Clients with higher levels of acceptance will have fully accepted their orientation and feel comfortable functioning normal lives. They will develop healthy, positive relationships and counseling such individuals requires treatment no different from any other client.

Substance Abuse

Substance abuse is a common societal concern addressed in counseling situations. Substance abuse can have a powerful impact on mental and physical functioning, and as a result it is classified as a mental disorder. In many cases, addictions and substance abuse problems are accompanied by additional mental disorders. One of the first steps for counselors to take is to understand themselves the complexity that arises when dealing with addiction and substance abuse issues. The effects of substance abuse are far ranging, affecting not only the social, mental, and physical well-being of the individual, but also their family, co-workers, friends, and others. Effective treatment requires not only bringing the individual to recognize the destructiveness of their addictions, but also helping them work through actually changing their habits, maintaining a drug-free lifestyle, and restoring positive, productive family and work relationships.

A basic understanding of some of the issues regarding substance abuse in the United States can be useful when considering substance abuse counseling. One of the groups that is most affected by substance abuse issues is adolescents and teens, for whom the growth rate of substance abuse is the largest. As time progresses, it becomes increasingly common for youths and teens to consume both alcohol and various forms of illegal drugs. The particularly worrisome factor in this trend is that fact that the average age at which a youth will first consume these substances is getting progressively younger.

By a wide margin, alcohol is the most abused substance by teens. Approximately half of all junior high and high school students in the United States drink on at least a monthly basis. And nearly 15 percent of teens admit to being intoxicated within the past year.

Although some people consider alcohol to be the least worrisome substance for teens to consume, the younger that an individual begins consuming it, the more likely they are to abuse it later in life. In addition, alcohol use has the potential to affect the cognitive development of an individual. Moving from alcohol to other forms of substance abuse, the most commonly used illegal drug among teens is marijuana (also called weed or pot). There is an increasing trend to view marijuana as an acceptable drug, especially due to the fact that it was popular among previous generations. Teens are also becoming increasingly likely to experiment with improper use of prescription drugs, inhalants, and cocaine (also called crack). These trends continue similarly on a nationwide scale for all ages. The most common addictive substances in the United States is nicotine (i.e., cigarettes), followed by alcohol, marijuana, and heroin.

The wide variety of drug use habits, motivations, and personal situations necessitate a varied approach to counseling individuals with substance abuse difficulties. Counseling must not only focus on stopping the initial use of drugs, but also on ensuring that the client will continue on in a healthy pattern of living. Tactics should be continually assessed and revised to ensure that the client's needs are being met effectively. There are a number of different methods which can be taken in regards to substance abuse counseling, including inpatient counseling, outpatient counseling, and private counseling.

Inpatient counseling describes actual facilities which individuals check into in which they are essentially forced to stop using the drug. Inpatient counseling can involve doctors, nurses, and physicians which monitor clients throughout the day, and counseling services for them to utilize while in the facility. This form of counseling often lasts for only a short period of time, and should therefore be followed up by additional counseling and supervision to ensure that the treatment lasts. Outpatient counseling similarly involves an appeal to an organization to help the individual to detoxify. However, in this case individuals continue to live among friends and relatives (i.e., they go about their normal lives) and meet with representatives on a regular basis to check up on their habits. During these meetings they may be given instructions or advice on how to upkeep a healthy lifestyle. Outpatient counseling also tends to be a short-term treatment plan. Finally, private counseling describes more formalized counseling services. It tends to have a more long-term and holistic approach, and can take place either individually, or in family or group settings.

The process of counseling individuals with substance abuse difficulties is similar in many ways to other forms of counseling. The first step is for a counselor to create a positive and trusting relationship with the client. Trust is an extremely important characteristic of substance abuse counseling, and counselors should strive to develop an accepting and honest atmosphere in counseling settings. Once trust has been developed, the counselor can begin to encourage client cooperation and investment in the counseling process. Unlike essentially all other forms of counseling, client support is not strictly necessary in substance abuse counseling (especially not in the early stages, where the main focus is on simply restricting or eliminating drug use). However, the more positive and invested the client is in the counseling, the more effective and successful it will be in the long run.

The client's motivations in counseling are important considerations, as they will by the primary driving factor throughout the process. By helping clients establish goals for themselves counselors can gain a better understanding of their underlying motives, and help them progress to healthier motives. Educating clients both about the risks and issues associated with drug use and about the resources available to those recovering from addictions can be helpful in engaging the client and their long-term success. Being supportive throughout the process, and ensuring that clients have an adequate support system, are both important ways that counselors can help maintain their clients' continued success. Because of the important of support when counseling individuals with substance abuse difficulties, family counseling and group counseling are highly recommended (and often preferred) forms of counseling.

The family members of those struggling with substance abuse are often the most affected by their behaviors. Involving them in the therapeutic process offers both a strong motivational force for the client and an immediate and relevant support system for them. However, in situations where substance abuse has led to violence or abuse towards family members, family counseling may not be appropriate or possible.

When it comes to matters of addictions, such as with alcohol and drug abusers, group therapy is a helpful and successful form of counseling. These group sessions can take two different forms: they can involve an independent group of individuals who meet together in a support-group setting with a qualified counselor, or they can involve a more directly psychoanalytical therapeutic approach based on educating individuals. In either case, the presence of a group can be helpful to alcohol and drug abusers for a number of reasons.

One reason for this is that it allows a sense of community to grow. It can be encouraging to those with substance abuse problems to know that they are not isolated from the rest of the world and that there are others who share similar difficulties. An open and communicative group therapy setting can allow individuals to regain and practice social skills and make lasting friendships to help them throughout the recovery process. Another reason that group counseling is typically preferred by alcohol and drug abusers is that it can allow them to see the progress that has been made my others, and be encouraged by it, as well as be able to encourage others. Although in many of their life situations the individuals may feel that no one really knows what they are going through, through group counseling sessions they can share their feelings more openly with people who have a direct understanding of the situation.

Polysubstance abuse is a condition in which an individual is addicted to or abusing three or more drugs on a regular basis over a period of 12 months. It occurs when the three types of drugs are used indiscriminately, meaning that there is no single drug that is considered a favorite or primary use drug, but rather they are all used relatively equally. Often polysubstance abuse begins as an attempt to amplify the characteristics of a particular drug, but leads to stronger addictions.

Polysubstance abuse is a useful term because many times if an individual is alternating between the three types of substances they may not qualify as dependent on, or abusing, any individual type of substance. However, when the three are considered jointly the addiction becomes more clearly manifest and identifiable.

Abuse

Another societal concern which counselors must often address is the issue of person abuse. The classification of abuse can be extended to a variety of harmful behaviors, including emotional, mental, and physical aspects. One of the first factors to be addressed is the fact that in situations where physical abuse is occurring, the counselor is not obligated to maintain client confidentiality. Rather, they should inform the proper authorities to ensure the protection of the client.

Although in some cases abusive relationships are clear cut and easily identified, in other cases it can be difficult to define. This is because abusive relationships typically develop gradually – particularly in cases of emotional abuse. Counseling in such situations requires involving all concerned parties, and raising an awareness of the problem. Once clients have recognized the effects and existence of the abusive behavior, then actions can be taken to begin reversing the effects of it.

Career Development

Within the field of counseling, the topic of career development is an important aspect to consider. Not only was vocational development the most important form of counseling in the development of the profession as a whole, but much of what counselors deal with in everyday client situations relates to jobs and careers. Part of the reason that career development is such a commonly addressed matter in counseling is because of the major role that it plays in identity formation. Because the average person will spend more than forty hours in a week working, a large portion of their lives revolves around the situations, people, and requirements associated with their job. Questions regarding an individual's profession are typically one of the first topics of conversation when introducing strangers. How a person does their work and the types of work they chose to do are ways in which people define themselves. Stated most simply, the work that a person does is integrally connected with who that person is.

The everyday importance of work in an individual's life has led to a continuing emphasis in the field of counseling on matters such as career development. As time has progressed, many different models for career development and career development counseling have emerged to respond to changing ideologies about and expectations of careers as a whole. These theories can be classified into a number of different types, including trait and factor approaches, decision approaches, sociological approaches, personality approaches, and developmental approaches. However, before any of these approaches can be discussed, some important vocabulary relevant to career development and counseling must be introduced.

One distinction that is commonly made in career development is an emphasis on the difference between a job, an occupation, and a career. A job is defined as the set of requirements that are associated with a specific position in an organization. Essentially, a job is the list of tasks that an individual is paid to perform. For example, a person who works as a bus boy in a restaurant may be required for their job to clear tables and do dishes. Similarly, a person who works as a secretary in an office may be required to type memos, file reports, or answer phone calls as a part of their job.

Because by its very nature the term job tends to be highly specific, the term occupation is used to refer to wider groups of similar jobs. For example, a professor, an elementary teacher, and a high school math teacher are all performing similar but distinct jobs. Therefore, they could all be classified under the occupational title of educator. Similarly, an astronomer, a physicist, and a molecular biologist may all be classified under the occupational title of scientist.

Finally, the term career is used to refer to the pathway which an individual takes relating to their work throughout their life. The terms job and occupation are different titles or work descriptions that a person may take on throughout their life while a career refers to the lifelong process of growth and accumulating experience. Some people consider the definition of career to refer specifically to the set of occupations with which an individual is involved, but others expand the definition to include avocational (i.e., leisure) activities and interests as well. Career development (which for all intents and purposes is synonymous with vocational or occupational development), then, involves a process of career education, decision making, and career guidance as the case may be.

Trait and Factor Theory

Returning to the different counseling approaches that can be used in career development, the oldest and most traditional method that has been used is known as the trait and factor theory or matching theory. The trait and factor theory is a theory which essentially involves classifying a person's individual characteristics. The basis of the theory is that all individuals can be characterized through a listing of their traits. Different types of aptitude tests, or simply general observations of the client and counselor, are used to determine the traits which the individual best embodies.

Correspondingly, different career options are also classified by the factors which are required to be most successful in that job. Successful application of this approach therefore requires that counselors have an extensive knowledge of the requirements of different jobs, and the factors that are required to be most successful in them. Once an analysis of traits and factors has been completed, the client is simply matched to the career for which they have the most similar profile (which is why this approach is also referred to as the matching theory). The underlying theory behind this approach is that the more traits and factors that are common between an individual and a job, the more suited the person will be to that job. Furthermore, if a person chooses a career path which is compatible with their personality traits, they will be more happy and successful in their career.

To successfully apply this method requires that a thorough and accurate examination of client's traits and job factors occurs. Because this approach essentially requires only that counselors know their client's well, the natural question becomes what about a client should be considered. Counselors may consider client's skills and abilities, financial and temporal needs, goals and desires, education level, family situation, lifestyle, or any other factors that they consider necessary to best understanding the client. This approach clearly requires the accumulation of a vast amount of knowledge both about the client and their possible career options. As a result of this, the method is used less and less frequently as the potential job market becomes increasingly diversified and the list of potential skills and characteristics increases along with it.

Decision Making

Decision approaches to career development involve the basic assumption that people choose their careers in a way that they believe will maximize the benefits to themselves and minimize the costs or losses. Although decision approaches attempt to quantify the decision making approach to the greatest extent possible, determining the benefits and costs of a particular career can be a rather subjective process. This is because such considerations involve both intrinsic and extrinsic factors. For example, the benefits of a particular job could include extrinsic motivators such as high pay, retirement plans, benefits packages, or others. However, the benefits of a particular job could also be intrinsic, such as an increase in social standing or a feeling of accomplishment.

Due to the amount of subjectivity involved in this approach, the primary strategy employed by counselors using decision approaches to career development is to first help clients identify the important decision points in their life, and then to empower them in making the most beneficial decisions. A myriad of decision approaches have developed, but they can largely be classified into two overarching types of theories which address different motivations which individuals have: expectancy theory and self-efficacy theory.

Expectancy theory is the belief that individuals base their decisions on a combination of their perceived competency and the value of the activity. Essentially the expectancy theory is an attempt to associate a mathematical model with the decision-making process. The theory claims that individuals will act only on the things that motivate them the most. The motivational factor is determined by considering the extent to which performing the task will result in a certain outcome then multiplying it by the value that they believe the task to hold. If a high enough "score" is generated, then the individual will perform the task; if a high enough "score" is not generated, then the individual will not perform the task. (Of course, people don't literally do calculations, the expectancy theory involves an intuitive or internal measurement system.)

As an example, consider an individual who is deciding whether or not to complete a report their boss asked them to write. They will consider first the extent to which their efforts will result in a well-written report. If they believe that working on the report will make it better this is a higher competency score. They will then consider whether or not writing the report is an important activity to complete. If they know they will get fired if they don't do it, they would assign it a high value score. Therefore, the individual would be highly motivated to work on the report. Because this system of motivation considers expectancy and value, career development theories based on the expectancy approach focus on the motivations and self-perceived talents of clients.

Albert Bandura

The most important theorist involved in self-efficacy theory is Albert Bandura. Bandura claimed that people are primarily motivated by their own perceptions of their ability to do a task well. Self-efficacy, then, is essentially the extent to which a person is confident in their ability. The more self-efficacious a person is, the longer they will work at a task and the more effort they will put into it. According to Bandura, self-efficacy is determined on a basis of four different factors; the four factors are past experiences, the experiences of others, current emotional status, and the feedback received from others.

Although self-efficacy and self-esteem may initially seem to be essentially the same, they are actually distinct measures of how a person perceives themselves. Self-esteem specifically refers to how a person perceives their self-worth. Self-efficacy, on the other hand, is a person's perception of their ability to complete a task. The two measures can coincide, but it is also possible for them to diverge (i.e., a person can have high self-esteem and low self-efficacy and they can alternatively have low self-esteem and high self-efficacy). Although it is important for a person to have a good sense of self-esteem, Bandura argued that self-efficacy was of central importance in an individual's life because it regulates how people spend their time, what things will motivate them, their cognitive and emotional responses to situations, and the work ethic.

To describe how self-efficacy is determined, Bandura proposed a triangular model incorporating three different elements: personal attributes, external factors, and behaviors. Because the development of self-efficacy is a lifelong process, Bandura focused on effectively applying these principles throughout childhood and development (though they are just as relevant in adults). Counseling based on Bandura's theories will focus on these factors when determining what career paths a person would be most suited to.

Sociological Approach

These approaches are also sometimes referred to as situational approaches, and argue that prior theories placed too little emphasis on the role of environmental factors in the career development process. Sociological approaches analyze the effect that barrier in a person's life restrict, or at the very least influence, their career possibilities. For example, those from low socioeconomic statuses generally do not exhibit the same potential for upward mobility as those from mid to high socioeconomic statuses. The situation in which a person lives and operates further influences their career decisions because it will affect their personality, education level, self-efficacy, behaviors, and other developmental factors of their life.

Personality Approach

Personality approaches are closely related to trait and factor approaches to the extent that they involve an analysis of an individual's personal traits; however, they are distinct because they involve little consideration of actual skills, traits, or factors, instead focusing purely on the personality of the client. There are two theories of specific importance in personality theory. These approaches are those attributed to Ann Roe and John Holland.

Ann Roe

The theory developed by Ann Roe emphasized three different factors in an individual's career development decisions. The first factor involves a consideration of needs. Roe's work was heavily influenced by Maslow's Theory of Self-Actualization in the sense that it focused on a hierarchy of needs. The lower-level needs related to physical and safety needs, the higher level needs related to social factors, and the highest level related to self-fulfillment.

The second important element that Roe considered was the relationship that a child had with their parent. According to Roe, this relationship would directly correlate with the types of need fulfillment that an individual would pursue later in their life. She argued that there were three potential relationships, each of which resulted in different career tendencies. One type of relationship focused on parenting involving emotional concentration on the child. Roe argued that this type of relationship was demanding and pressuring. While the child's lower level needs would be satisfied, higher-level needs would be neglected. Therefore, Roe believed that individuals raised in this type of situation would seek satisfaction of the mid-level social needs (such as emotional fulfillment and belonging) through their jobs.

The second type of situation that Roe identified is described as avoidance of the child. In this parenting relationship both the physical and emotional needs of the child are not met. Roe argued that as a result, individuals raised in this type of situation will seek fulfillment of lower-level needs relating to material factors (i.e., they will focus on pay, social status, material benefits, etc.) through their job choices.

The third situation which Roe identified is referred to as acceptance of the child. When this type of parental relationship is established, both physical needs and social and emotional needs of the child are fulfilled by their parents. This allows a development process which facilitates seeking the highest-level needs later in life. Individuals raised in this situation will be able to make career development decisions which will give them a sense of fulfillment and achievement in their lives.

In addition to the consideration of different need levels and parental relationships, the third factor which Roe identified as important in career development is genetics. Roe argued that every individual is born with a set of unique talents and skills that will impact their future career options and preferences. These genetic endowments in combination with the other two factors will lead people as they make their career decisions. In regards to genetic endowments, people will choose fields that are most compatible with their abilities. For example, Roe identified business, service, technology, science, organization, culture, and other areas. Then, based on the need seeking patterns which people exhibit they will pick careers with varying levels of responsibility involvement, which Roe described based on a scale ranging from unskilled, to semiskilled, to professional in varying stages.

John Holland

The second personality-based approach was created by John Holland, and is used even more commonly than is Roe's model. Holland's model can be summarized by two overarching principles. Firstly, all people can be categorized on a basis of six different personality types, as can all jobs or work situations. Secondly, people's behaviors are influenced based on interactions with their environments, and people will choose environments to work in that are most similarly matched to their own personalities.

The six personality types which Holland identified are realistic, investigative, artistic, social, technical, and conventional. Realistic individuals excel in areas that involve manual work. The key traits of this category include practicality, working with hands, stability, and masculinity. Realistic individuals value predictability and power. Occupations, falling within this category include farming, construction, or other activity-based work fields. The investigative category is characterized by a more knowledge-based (rather than activity-based) approach. Key traits of the investigative category include intellectualism, and a love of critical or analytical thinking. Investigative individuals value recognition and status, and prize the ability to think in terms of and manipulate abstractions. As a result, occupations most suited to investigative individuals include programming or any form of scientist or doctor.

The next personality category, artistic individuals, is characterized by an open and creative approach. These individuals tend to be much more aesthetically minded and emotional. Therefore, the key features of this personality type include spontaneity, expressiveness, and artistic tendencies. For example, artists, musicians, writers, and designers are all occupations well-suited to individuals with an artistic personality. The fourth category, social individuals, describes individuals who are focused on relationships, and enjoy working with (and especially helping) others. Key traits of social personalities are a cooperative and friendly nature, supportive and empathetic disposition, and an avoidance of technical skills. Examples of fields well suited to individuals with a social personality include any form of counseling or public service.

The fifth personality type, enterprising, is used to describe ambitious and leadership-oriented individuals. Enterprising individuals are high energy and adventurous. They are natural leaders with dominant, persuasive personalities. Fields which individuals with enterprising personality types are most suited to include lawyers, businesspersons, and politicians. The final personality type, conventional personality, describes individuals with a rule-oriented, structured view of life. Conventional individuals value efficiency, self-control, and dependability. These individuals will flourish in environments which allow specificity, such as secretarial work or fields involving data entry or organization (although not analysis).

In addition to classifying each of these six personality types, Holland also ordered them into a hexagonal chart. This chart has come to be known as the RIASEC model (each letter represents one of the six personality types), and plots the personality types in a pinwheel fashion. Adjacent personality types (such as realistic and intellectual) are more common with each other than those standing opposite them. Because it is highly unlikely that an individual's personality could be narrowed into a single type, Holland's model involves assigning individuals three-letter codes based on their traits. The more similar the three personality types a person is assigned are, the more they are said to be consistent. The spread between the first two letters is considered to be a measure of differentiation (the greater the spread, the more differentiated the individual). According to Holland, in order for an individual to exhibit the maximum amount of satisfaction and efficiency in their work life, it is necessary for them to achieve congruence. In other words, their work situation needs to match with their personality.

The reason that Holland's theory is one of the most popular career development theories is that it is quite simple to use. Holland developed a classification of over four hundred careers on a basis of the three-letter system, which allows individuals to simply compare their own personality to this list of careers and determine which one their personality is most suited for. However, one of the drawbacks of this system is that it doesn't go into great depth with the career development process; instead, it focuses primarily on the immediate decision-making process.

 Developmental Approaches

The developmental approaches are distinct from other approaches because of their intense focus on career development as a process rather than an act. The two most notable theories that take developmental approaches are those of Eli Ginzberg and Donald Super.

Ginzberg's theory divides the career development process into three important phases: fantasy, tentative, and realistic. The fantasy phase lasts throughout a person's childhood, ending around age 11. In this phase, an individual has only an abstract concept of the working world, and their plan for their future career will shift from one occupation to the next based on idealized perceptions. The decisions and perceptions formed in this stage aren't typically lasting due to the fact that they involve considerations of job reality, time perspective, or abilities and potentials that are central factors in making career decisions.

The second phase, the tentative phase, lasts from the end of the fantasy phase around age 11 to approximately age 17. During this phase, individuals first gain more information about the various careers available to them. They will begin to have a more realistic perspective of the need to obtain a job and the requirements that come along with different jobs. Towards the end of the phase, the individual becomes increasingly aware of the fulfillment potential offered by work, rather than the material aspects of money and status. This phase is marked by a sense of urgency to make decisions about a career.

The final phase, the realistic phase, involves actually progressing into a job situation. Ginzberg posited that this phase lasted from approximately ages 18 to 21. During this phase individuals will more thoroughly explore various career options. Through this process of exploration, their career goals and ambitions will begin to crystallize as they chose their future career. This process of committing to a certain career was described by Ginzberg as specification and he actually argued later that complete specification never occurred, as individuals make important career decisions and adjustments throughout their lives.

Donald Super

The second important developmental approach was developed by Donald Super. Super's theory essentially built on Ginzberg's. It divided the stages more distinctly, extended them to last throughout an individual's life, and provided clarification about the final stages. Super's developmental theory and Holland's personality theory are by far the two most referenced theories in the field of career development counseling today. Super's theory can be broken down into three major concepts: life stages, vocational self-concept, and career maturity.

Super broke the career development process into five life stages: growth, exploration, establishment, maintenance, and decline. The growth phase (age 0-14) essentially incorporates Ginzberg's fantasy phase. In the growth phase, individuals develop their own self-concept and are first introduced to the world of work. The exploration phase (age 15-24) is characterized by a tentative exploration of various career fields, such as by taking different classes in school, or independently learning about different career fields. During this phase a career preference begins to crystallize and individuals will begin implementing this preference as they enter the working world. The establishment phase (ages 24-44) involves a stabilization of career preferences and advancement in the chosen career. The individual starts this phase at entry-level positions, but works their way into a more stabilized position as they gain experience. The maintenance phase (age 45-64) involves retaining the status that has been achieved to this point. It involves making continual career adjustments to either improve or preserve status. The final stage, decline (ages 65+) is characterized by disengaging from the career and moving into retirement.

The second major component of Super's theories is the development of a vocational self-concept. This vocational self-concept is essentially a combination of an individual's beliefs about their own capabilities and preferences, and the skills and demands of various vocations. It additionally incorporates their self-image and self-esteem. Career choices, then, are an expression of one's vocational self-concept. This vocational self-concept develops through life as education and experience grow. Accordingly, an important role of counselors is to help clients correctly identify and interpret these factors as they relate to career decisions.

The third major component of Super's theories is the idea of career maturity. Most simply, career maturity is a measure of the extent to which a person has progressed through the career development process. Super argued that each of the stages must occur in order, and the extent to which a person has acclimated to the stage that they are can be described as career maturity. Essentially, career maturity is an abstract measure of how well suited an individual is to their current stage of life.

Career Education

Each of these different approaches to career development (trait and factor, decisional, personality, or developmental) can be applied by counselors as they see fit when helping individuals in making career decisions. In additional to basic counseling, however, career counseling also involves a fair amount of career education. One of the underlying assumptions of career counseling is that individuals, left to their own devices, either cannot or will not gather sufficient information regarding career options. This could be a result of either a sincere lack of access to information, or a lack of understanding the importance of gathering the information. In either case, one of the primary roles of counselors is to increase their client's exposure to different career options.

One of the most important contexts in which career education occurs is in school environments. Because all students have a pressing need to gain information about career options, opportunities such as careers classes, job exploration activities, and discussions with counselors about options are a regular part of the educational process. Students, however, are not the only ones in need of career education, and career education is also an important part of the career development process for many adults.

At any age, career education typically occurs through two different methods: direct contact and through dispersal of information. The direct contact approach involves gaining some form of actual experience with different careers. At this most basic level, this experience could come from simply speaking with or interviewing an individual who holds a particular job. This allows clients to gain honest and realistic information about the position. At levels of deeper involvement, direct contact approaches can include "job shadowing" days or even temporary internships.

While direct contact approaches are typically considered the best way to gain information about occupations, they require significant investments of time, energy, and resources. As a result, the more common approach is the dispersal of information. To accommodate adults seeking career education, governments, businesses, agencies, and others are striving to make information increasingly available. Although in the past most information existed in printed form, the use of technology has allowed information to become much more easily accessed and circulated. Scores of databases and websites can be accessed which give information about career options and detail everything from the educational requirements to typical working environments to average pay. Through the combined efforts of career counseling approaches and career education, clients can find increasing satisfaction with their working life, which will allow them to lead more fulfilling lives overall.

 Human Development

Over the years, many different theorists and theories have contributed various different theories regarding the development process. In a general sense, there are two different types of development which counselors study: personal development and social development. Personal development deals with the cognitive, individual development that a person goes through. Social development is more focused on behavioral aspects of development. Some of the most important developmental theories were created by Erik Erikson, Jean Piaget, Abraham Maslow, Sigmund Freud, and Albert Bandura.

Erik Erikson was a psychoanalyst who created stages of emotional growth in regards to human babies. Each stage has different needs and lessons to be learned. If the child or infant does not learn that lesson, he may have a harder time in life down the road. For example, if a baby is crying constantly and is not taken care of, or if it is ignored, it can come to feel mistrust toward others. Another example is the young adult stage.

The young adult must deal with either being intimate with someone or deal with feeling isolated. According to Erikson, the most important thing is the development of trust.

Infant *Trust vs. Mistrust*
Infants gain trust and confidence from their caregivers. If those caregivers are warm and responsive then they will know that the world is good.

Toddler *Autonomy vs. Shame and Doubt*
Children want to choose and decide things for themselves. Autonomy is when the parents give the child that necessary free reign over their choices.

Preschooler *Initiative vs. Guilt*
By playing make-believe the child discovers who they are and who they can become. They can try their hand at being a princess or a mother or father to their dolls.

School-Age Child *Industry vs. Inferiority*
Children learn to work and get along with each other. Inferiority develops from negative social situations.

Adolescent *Identity vs. Role Confusion*
The adolescent tries many roles to answer the question "Who am I?" and "Where do I fit in society?"

Young Adult *Intimacy vs. Isolation*
Young adults work to create emotional ties and relationships to others. Because of earlier trust issues, some young adults cannot form these attachments and it leaves them isolated.

Middle-Age Adult *Generativity vs. Stagnation*
Generativity deals with leaving something for the next generation. Those that do not do this feel an absence of accomplishment.

Old Age *Ego Integrity vs. Despair*
In this stage, people think about the person that they have become. Integrity comes from achieving what one wanted in life. For those that are unhappy with their past, despair results in fear of death.

Instinct Theory

Instinct theory is a theory of motivation attempting to explain human behavior. Ac- cording to instinct theory, human behavior is driven by biological instincts. All organisms are genetically programmed with tendencies that help them survive. These instincts are present at birth (not learned behaviors) and they tend to be universal, like birds migrating for the winter, salmon swimming hundreds of miles upstream to mate, or the rooting reflex that helps infants seek out nourishment.

Psychologist William McDougall was one of the first to write about instinct theory. He defined an instinct as a behavior that is A) unlearned, B) uniform in expression, and C) universal in a species. He outlined 18 instincts including curiosity, the maternal instinct, laughter, comfort, sex, and hunger. Another psychologist William James offered different instincts such as attachment, play, anger, fear, shyness, modesty, love, shame, and cleanliness. One psychologist, Luther Lee Bernard, counted 5,759 primary instincts.

Psychologist's disability to agree on a number of instincts is one of several criticisms of instinct theory. Another is that not all behaviors can be explained by instincts. Instinct theory also does not explain why the same instincts produce different behaviors in different people, why some instincts appear in some instances but not in others, or the instincts themselves.

Jean Piaget

Jean Piaget (1896-1980) was a biologist who originally studied mollusks (publishing twenty scientific papers on them by the time he was 21), but moved into the study of the development of children's understanding, through observing them and talking and listening to them while they worked on exercises he set. His view of how children's minds work and develop has been enormously influential, particularly in educational theory. His particular insight was the role of maturation (simply growing up) in children's increasing capacity to understand their world; children cannot undertake certain tasks until they are psychologically mature enough to do so. His research spawned a great deal more study, much of which has undermined the detail of his own, but like many other investigators, his importance comes from his overall vision.

Piaget proposed that children's thinking does not develop entirely smoothly: instead, there are certain points at which it 'takes off' and moves into completely new areas and capabilities. He saw these transitions as taking place at about 18 months, 7 years and 11 or 12 years. This has been taken to mean that, before these ages, children are not capable (no matter how bright) of understanding things in certain ways, and has been used as the basis for scheduling the school curriculum (Atherton, 2002). Piaget is a **cognitive theorist.** Piaget believed that the individual actively constructs knowledge about the world.

 Piaget's Relevant Definitions

ASSIMILATION
The process by which a person takes material into their mind from the environment, which may mean changing the evidence of their senses to make it fit.

ACCOMMODATION
The difference made to one's mind or concepts by the process of assimilation. Note that assimilation and accommodation go together. You can't have one without the other.

CLASSIFICATION
The ability to group objects together on the basis of common features.

CLASS INCLUSION
The understanding of more advanced than simple classification, that some classes or sets of objects are also sub-sets of a larger class. (e.g., there is a class of objects called dogs. There is also a class called animals. But all dogs are also animals, so the class of animals includes that of dogs).

CONSERVATION
The realization that objects or sets of objects stay the same even when they are changed about or made to look different. For example, children can understand that the same amount of liquid is in two different shaped jars.

DEVELOPMENTAL NORM
A statistical measure of typical scores for categories of information.

EGOCENTRISM

The belief that you are the center of the universe and everything revolves around you: the corresponding inability to see the world as someone else does and adapt to it. Not moral "selfishness", just an early stage of psychological development. The move away from egocentrism is called decentration.

ELABORATION

Relating new information to something familiar. An example would be learning how to cook a pasta dish. You may have cooked something similar in the past. In your mind you may think, "This is like that time I made Ramen except now I do…"

OPERATION

The process of working something out in your head. Young children (in the sensorimotor and pre-operational stages) have to act and try things out in the real world to work things out (like count on fingers). Older children and adults can do more in their heads.

RECOGNITION

The ability to identify correctly something encountered before.

RECALL

Being able to reproduce knowledge from memory.

SCHEMA (OR SCHEME)

The representation in the mind of a set of perceptions, ideas, and/or actions, which go together.

STAGE

A period in a child's development in which he or she is capable of understanding some things but not others.

 # Piaget's Stages of Development

This table was created by James Atherton and defines the different developmental stages according to Jean Piaget.

Developmental Stage and Approximate Age	Characteristic Behavior
Sensory Motor Period (0-24 months)	
Reflexive Stage (0-2 months)	Simple reflex activity such as grasping and sucking.
Primary Circular Reactions (2-4 months)	Reflexive behaviors occur in stereotyped repetition such as opening and closing fingers repetitively.
Secondary Circular Reactions (4-8 months)	Repetition of actions to reproduce interesting consequences such as kicking one's feet to move a mobile suspended over the crib.
Coordination of Secondary Reactions (8-12 months)	Responses become coordinated into more complex sequences. Actions take on an "intentional" character such as the infant reaches behind a screen to obtain a hidden object.
Tertiary Circular Reactions (12-18 months)	Discovery of new ways to produce the same consequence or obtain the same goal such as the infant pulling a pillow toward him in an attempt to get a toy resting on it.
Invention of New Means Through Mental Combination (18-24 months)	Evidence of an internal representational system. Symbolizing the problem-solving sequence before actually responding. Deferred imitation.
The Preoperational Period (2-7 years)	
Preoperational Phase (2-4 years)	Increased use of verbal representation but speech is egocentric. The beginnings of symbolic rather than simple motor play. Transductive reasoning. Can think about something without the object being present by use of language.

Intuitive Phase (4-7 years)	Speech becomes more social, less egocentric. The child has an intuitive grasp of logical concepts in some areas. However, there is still a tendency to focus attention on one aspect of an object while ignoring others. Concepts formed are crude and irreversible. Easy to believe in magical increase, decrease, disappearance. Reality not firm. Perceptions dominate judgment. In the moral-ethical realm, the child is not able to show principles underlying best behavior. Rules of a game cannot develop in the mind; only uses simple do's and do not's imposed by authority.

Period of Concrete Operations (7-11 years)
Evidence for organized, logical thought. There is the ability to perform multiple classification tasks, order objects in a logical sequence, and comprehend the principle of conservation. Thinking becomes less transductive and less egocentric. The child is capable of concrete problem solving. Some reversibility now possible (quantities moved can be restored such as in arithmetic: 3+4 = 7 and 7-4 = 3, etc.) Classifying logic-finding bases to sort unlike objects into logical groups where previously it was on superficial perceived attributes such as color. Categorical labels such as "number" or "animal" now available.

Period of Formal Operations (11-15 years)
Thought becomes more abstract, incorporating the principles of formal logic. The ability to generate abstract propositions, multiple hypotheses and their possible outcomes is evident. Thinking becomes less tied to concrete reality. Formal logical systems can be acquired. Can handle proportions, algebraic manipulation, and other purely abstract processes. If $a + b = x$ then $x = a - b$. If $ma/ca = IQ = 1.00$ then $Ma = CA$. Prepositional logic present, in as-if and if-then steps. Can use aids such as axioms to transcend human limits on comprehension. Can think hypothetically and test hypothesis. Based on the information in these stages, you can see it is important to have age appropriate materials in school.

Piaget and Freud both agreed that environmental influences could affect the time spent in stages but not the order.

 Maslow's Hierarchy of Needs

A third important individual in the field of development is Abraham Maslow. Maslow believed that there were five stages of needs that defined how a person behaved and responded in different situations. His theory has been termed Maslow's Hierarchy of Needs, and has been very influential both in its pure form and in the sense that it has influenced many of the theories which followed it.

Maslow's Hierarchy of Needs consists of the following stages, from the top down:

- Self-actualization
- Esteem needs
- Belonging and love
- Safety
- Physical needs

These stages begin at physical needs. An individual first needs to have food, water, and shelter before they can worry about other things. If a person does not have these needs met, then all of their energies will be focused on obtaining them. These are the most basic needs that a person can have filled.

Once those needs are met, an individual may start to think of other needs such as safety. Aside from physical needs which sustain life, safety is the next most important focus of any individual. For example, safety needs may involve purchasing a gun or moving to a more prosperous and safe area.

Once the physical and safety needs are both met (i.e., a person is fed, clothed and safe), Maslow posited that individuals will want to meet needs of belonging and love through relationships. An individual in this third stage of development will seek out relationships with others. This could involve finding friendships with co-workers, entering into a committed relationship, or spending time with family. Any needs related to an individual's social standing with others would fall into this category of needs.

Moving onto the Maslow's fourth stage, esteem needs, once an individual feels loved they may begin to focus on their self-esteem. These needs include how they feel as a person, and what they are contributing to their environments. At this stage, individuals are highly aware of the opinions of those around them, and their actions are motivated by a need to be accepted. For many people, this is the highest stage that they ever reach; however, Maslow argued that the highest stage which a person can attain is self-actualization.

The final stage, self-actualization, describes individuals who are entirely comfortable with themselves, and focused on personal growth and achievement rather than on gaining approval from others.

Maslow believed that a person would progress through these stages chronologically. In other words, he believed that people cannot skip a step. In order to achieve self-actualization, for example, an individual must first satisfy their self-esteem needs.

Freud's Psychosexual Stages

The fourth important developmental theory to be aware of is Freud's psychosexual stages. Freud believed that human actions are dictated by unconscious motives (i.e., the id, ego, and superego). Further he argued that the unconscious mind was primarily influenced by sexual motivations. He therefore theorized a system which describes five different stages of development which correspond to different sexual impulses. These stages are oral, anal, phallic, latency, and genital. The five stages are described in the table below.

Stage	Age	Description
Oral	Birth-1 Year	The new ego directs the baby's sucking activities toward breast or bottle. If oral needs are not met appropriately, the individual may develop such habits as thumb sucking, fingernail biting, pencil chewing, overeating and smoking.
Anal	1-3 Years	Young toddlers and preschoolers enjoy holding and releasing urine and feces. Toilet training becomes a major issue between parent and child. If parents insist that children be trained before they are ready or make too few demands, conflicts about anal control may appear in the form of extreme orderliness and cleanliness or messiness and disorder.

Phallic	3-6 Years	Id impulses transfer to the genitals, and the child finds pleasure in genital stimulation. Freud's Oedipus Conflict for boys and Electra Conflict for girls take place. Young children feel a sexual desire for the other-sex parent. To avoid punishment, they give up this desire and instead adopt the same-sex parent's characteristics and values. As a result, the superego is formed and children feel guilty each time they violate its standards. The relationships between id, ego and superego established at this time determine the individual's basic personality orientation.
Latency	6-11 years	Sexual instincts die down, and the superego develops further. The child acquires new social values from adults outside the family and from play with same-sex peers.
Genital	Adolescence	Puberty causes the sexual impulses of the phallic stage to reappear. If development has been successful during earlier stages, it leads to marriage, mature sexuality, and the birth and rearing of children.

Karen Horney

Karen Horney was born in Germany on September 16, 1885. When she was nine years old, Karen developed a crush on her brother. His rejection of her was the initial cause of the depression that she suffered for the rest of her life. In 1906, Horney entered medical school against her parent's wishes. There she met Oscar Horney, who she married in 1909. She graduated with her medical degree from the University of Berlin in 1913. For a while she studied Freudian theory and explored psychoanalytic theories with Karl Abraham. After four years, she began analyzing patients at the Berlin Psychoanalytic Clinic.

When her husband's business shut down and he developed meningitis, she moved without him to the United States with their three daughters. There she became friends with other notable intellectuals and developed her theories on psychology.

Horney's theory of neurosis is her most prominent theory. She saw neurosis in a way others did not. Instead of abuse or neglect, Horney named cause of neurosis in adulthood to be parental indifference, which she referred to as the "basic evil." She also saw neurosis as a coping technique and a relatively normal experience. She explained that the needs felt by a neurotic are felt by everybody to some extent, but a neurotic's need for these things is much more intense. A person with neurosis will experience great anxiety if their needs are not met. Horney described ten neuroses, including:

1. The need for acceptance and affection
2. Love and intimacy
3. Simplicity
4. Power
5. The need to manipulate
6. Social recognition
7. Admiration
8. Personal accomplishment
9. Independence
10. Perfection

She later identified three main coping strategies found within the ten neuroses: compliance (moving towards others) aggression (moving against others) and withdrawal (moving away from others).

Horney also had several Neo-Freudian theories, most of which developed from her disagreement with Freud's theories on female psychology. She rejected his concept of "penis envy" and proposed the concept of "womb envy" in which men feel inferior because they cannot have children. She theorized that men's drive to succeed in the workplace stemmed from this feeling of inferiority.

Horney also did not believe that sex and aggression drive personality. She suggested (instead of Freud's Oedipus complex) that clinging to one parent and jealousy of the other was caused by a disrupted parent-child relationship. Horney's refutation of Freud's theories about women generated more interest in female psychology. Horney also believed that each person has a personal role in their own mental health. In 1942, she published her book Self-Analysis, in which she discussed the neuroses, psychoanalysis, and how individuals can take advantage of psychoanalytic techniques personally. Horney often encouraged self-analysis and self-help. She believed that, regarding relatively minor neurotic problems, people could be their own psychiatrists.

Kohlberg's Theory of Moral Development

Level 1: Preconventional morality

Stage 1: Punishment and obedience phase. Whether you will be punished or not determines what is moral or not. For example, you don't speed when driving the car because you know that you might get a ticket, a negative sanction from an authority figure.

Stage 2: A person becomes aware of two different viewpoints. You see the right action as what satisfies your personal needs. You don't speed while driving a car because you want the lower rates on car insurance that you will get having no tickets on your record.

Level 2: Conventional morality

Stage 3: A "good boy-good girl" orientation. You do what is right in order to gain status or approval from other people or society. For example, you don't get speeding tickets while driving because in your circle of friends that would make you appear irresponsible, therefore lowering your social status.

Stage 4: Social-order-maintaining orientation. A person abides by the law because they think that law is a higher order. It is their duty as a responsible citizen to not speed. This type of person would not run a red light in a deserted intersection even if he had been waiting five minutes. They believe that laws cannot be broken under any circumstance.

Level 3: Postconventional morality

Stage 5: The social contract orientation. A person is concerned with how their action might affect society. "I'm not going to speed because I might get into an accident and injure someone."

Stage 6: The universal ethical principle orientation. A person makes decisions according to his or her conscience. Not many, if any, people get to this stage.

Kohlberg believed that you go through these stages one at a time and cannot skip them. According to both Kohlberg and Piaget, the most immature reason to do something is to avoid punishment.

 Carol Gilligan

Carol Gilligan was born in New York City on November 28, 1936. She received her master's degree in psychology from Radcliffe in 1960 and her PhD in psychology from Harvard in 1964. Three years later, Gilligan began teaching at Harvard. There, she worked as a research assistant under Lawrence Kohlberg, known for his theory of moral development. Gilligan herself focused on the moral development of women. Gilligan is known as the founder of gender difference psychology, which focuses on the differences between how men and women think. According to Gilligan, these differences arise from social influences and gender conditioning. Gilligan was also one of the founders of the ethics of care, which emphasizes the importance of emotional response in moral decision-making. Proponents of ethics of care believe that emotions allow us to grasp a situation that the "justice perspective" may not. Gilligan's theories put her at the front of the feminist movement.

Gilligan's adaptation of Lawrence Kohlberg's theory of moral development for women is her best-known contribution to psychology. In Kholberg's theory of moral development, the guiding principles of the highest level of moral reasoning are justice and individual rights. Kohlberg found that men tend to focus on justice, and that more men reach the highest stage than women. Gilligan argued that Kholberg's theory was biased towards men.

In 1982, she published *In a Different Voice: Psychological Theory and Women's Development,* which criticizes Kohlberg's theory and gives her own views on female morality. According to Gilligan, men and women have equal moral status, but women place stronger emphasis on relationships and caring in moral decision making. They tend to base their moral foundation on how their decisions will affect others. Gilligan adapted Kholberg's stages to better represent her research into female moral reasoning.

The stages are:

Preconventional morality – During this stage, there is a strong focus on survival and self-interest.

Conventional – During this stage, women prioritize selflessness and caring about others.

Postconventional – In the final stage of moral development, women emphasize taking responsibility for the consequences of their choices and gaining control of their own lives. Caring for others is a strong component of this high stage of moral development.

Social Learning Theory

Bandura believed that traditional instruction and reinforcement patterns were not the only way that people learned, but that observation of others was also an important factor of the learning process.

The social learning theory consists of three major premises. The first is that people can learn through observation. Bandura identified three different ways that this learning can occur: live, or through direct observation; verbal, or through descriptions of actions; and symbolic, or via media such as television or radio. Bandura demonstrated that it was in fact possible for people to learn through observations through experiments in which children viewed adults treating a doll violently. When left alone the children would often imitate, or model, the behavior that they had seen.

The second premise of the social learning theory is that factors other than those that are external are important in learning. In other words, there are intrinsic reinforcers, such as pride, acceptance, and happiness, which can be just as instrumental in the learning process. In this way a person's environment can affect their learning because many of these reinforces are generated through contact with others.

The final premise of the social learning theory is that learning does not always result in changing behavior. Though many theories such as cognitive and behavioral theories operate on the basis that teaching more correct principles will lead innately to better behavior or thought processes, Bandura argued that there are many factors which influence whether or not a person demonstrates the traits that are learned.

Counseling Today

In addition to understanding these major theories, a number of other general debates and concerns arise in counseling regarding development. For example, the fact that it is easier to take counseling as a child than an adult is relevant to discussions of development. Several arguments are given as to why it is better to take counseling at a younger age. One of the most important reasons that it is better to get counseling earlier in life is that children's minds are more impressionable, and the older a person gets the harder it becomes for them to change. It can also be more difficult to identify problems and their roots when a patient, as an adult, has had a lifetime to ignore, suppress, or avoid them. Also, if a problem remains unsolved throughout childhood, it can have a significant impact on the individual's psychological and sociological growth and development.

Another developmental issue that is often raised in counseling is as to whether boys and girls tend to have different characteristics as a result of developmental differences or whether it should be attributed to how they are raised. On the one hand, there are many people who advocate the perspective that differences between genders are a result of fundamental differences that people are born with. On the other hand, there are many who argue that gender differences emerge as a result of cultural norms that children learn as they grow. Commonly referred to as the Nature vs. Nurture debate, there is really no definitive answer to which side is correct. Rather, there is evidence which supports both theories.

The actual neurological differences between male and female infants are fairly insignificant (though they do exist). However, by simply walking into a kindergarten classroom it is easy to see that there are fundamental differences in the way that each behaves. In learning, girls tend to excel when they can relate things to their own lives or the real world, whereas boys tend to excel with a more mechanical and mathematical approach. In addition, boys tend to be more open to using various learning approaches. This doesn't mean that boys are inherently smarter, simply that the two genders excel in different situations. Also, these differences in gender tend to lessen as they age (i.e., the differences are much less exaggerated in a high school classroom than a kindergarten classroom).

This doesn't mean that gender differences arise singly from inborn differences. There can be little doubt that at least part of the reason for gender differences lays in the way that children are raised. Typically girls will be dressed in more feminine pinks and purples, and they will be given toys such as dolls or kitchen sets. Boys will be dressed in blues and reds, and they will be given toys such as trucks or monsters. In addition to this, movies, music, and storybooks all reinforce the typical gender stereotypes.

Assessment & Appraisal Techniques

Often when people think about the counseling process, their first thoughts are to imagine sitting in a room and having endless discussions with a counselor. While face-to-face interactions and discussions are an important part of the counseling process, assessment and appraisal are also necessary tools for an effective counselor to employ when working with clients. The most basic level of assessment involves test giving; however, there is actually much more involved with the process of assessment than simply scoring tests.

Understanding the assessment process requires definitions of terms related to the process, including assessment, measurement, evaluation, appraisal, interpretation, and testing. Assessment is best thought of as a process. Although in a school setting the term assessment is often used synonymously with test, in counseling the two are quite different. Assessment is a multidimensional approach to diagnosis which requires incorporating information gathered from tests, from discussions, from observations, and from many other possible sources.

The assessment process can be broken down into four basic steps. First, the purpose of counseling must be identified. At this stage of the process, the client and counselor will begin to build a relationship, and the problem for which they need counseling will be identified. This may involve the counselor diagnosing the problem for the client (i.e., the medical model), or it may involve the client identifying their objectives and concerns. At this point a spectrum or range of potential issues is identified.

The second step of the assessment process is to clarify the situation. Here the list of potential issues is narrowed down into those that the counseling will most specifically focus on. This is done as the counselor is able to continue gaining information about the client and their problems. The counselor will also discuss and clarify the goals and expectations that the client has for the counseling. In some situations it is possible for multiple concerns to be addressed simultaneously, but in many cases it is simpler and more helpful to rank the list of concerns and address the most important ones first. Concerns receive higher rankings if they are of immediate concern to the client, can be addressed quickly, have the most adverse effect on the client, or must be resolved before other concerns can be addressed.

The third step of the process is to determine how to proceed with counseling. At this stage of the process the counselor will identify specifically what will be done in terms of counseling activities, and they will identify how progress will be measured and determined. It is important that measurement methods are determined at the beginning of the counseling process so that progress can be determined effectively and without bias. This helps additionally clarify objectives for the client and helps them understand what is expected of them through the process as well.

At this stage it is important that the counselor comes to an understanding of what the client expects from the counseling process. To determine how progress should be measured, the counselor should ask the client what they considered to be acceptable evidence of improvement. For example, a person who is suffering from depression may consider crying less often to be an acceptable indicator. Similarly, a person who is suffering from anxiety may consider feeling more relaxed an acceptable standard. Determining client expectations can shape the procedures and focuses of the process, and are important to consider for this reason.

Finally, the fourth step of the assessment process involves actually implementing the practices and procedures that were identified in step three. Based on the success or failure of different counseling activities, the process may be altered to suit the client better, or additional concerns may be raised and addressed.

In contrast to assessment, the term testing is used to describe a specific event. Essentially tests are a snapshot in time which is used to quickly and concisely gather information about a client. A test may be in multiple-choice, fill-in-the-blank, rating, short answer, or another format. The point is that testing describes the physical situation of answering questions. These questions are used by counselors as a form of measurement. Measurement in counseling refers to an attempt to use the results of a test to quantify or describe certain traits, characteristics, or behaviors that clients may exhibit. Measurement aids counselors in conceptualizing and defining client behaviors.

The measurements that are gleaned from tests are then used by counselors to evaluate the client's situation. Evaluation, used synonymously with appraisal, is the process of using the measurements gained from testing and comparing them to standards to determine whether the client's behaviors are abnormal or appropriate. Through evaluating the results of testing, counselors can then interpret the information to come to a diagnosis. Interpretation is a critical step in the process because an incorrect interpretation renders the assessment process as a whole invalid.

Although testing is not the only aspect of assessment, it can be an important and useful source of information for counselors. Therefore, understanding different elements related to testing is useful in counseling situations. One important aspect of testing to understand is the difference between standardized and non-standardized tests. Tests can be either standardized or non-standardized, and depending on the specific situation either form of testing can be useful.

Standardized tests involve specific procedures and formats. They are well tested and their meanings are therefore safe to be generalized. Standardized tests are the types of tests that most people are familiar with today. They allow counselors to make simple comparisons based on scores to determine what course of action will likely be the most effect. Non-standardized tests, on the other hand, do not meet these criteria. Because of this, they are much more informal and cannot be generalized.

Standardized tests can be used to gather information to be used in assessment in two major areas: the cognitive domain and the affective domain. The cognitive domain refers to areas involving intellectual skills. This could involve factors such as simple fact recollection to assessment on a more complex level. General intelligence measures, aptitude tests, and standardized achievement tests (such as those used in school testing) are all examples of standardized tests which focus on the cognitive domain. Of these, aptitude tests are some of the most important tests used in counseling, especially in the field of career counseling.

Aptitude tests are analytically based tests which are designed to assess the takers abilities in a variety of different areas. In the field of career counseling aptitude tests are often used to gather information about a person and what their interests or skills are. The individual can then be guided to appropriate jobs for their personalities. Aptitude tests are also often used by organizations in screening potential employees. They can be based on anything from numeric abilities, abstract reasoning, mechanical knowledge or any other information considered important to the employer. Individuals should work to be well prepared for aptitude tests, as they may make the difference in obtaining a job or promotion, and may set them apart from the crowd.

The second branch of standardized tests focuses on the affective domain. The affective domain has its focus in non-cognitive understanding. Where the cognitive domain focuses on intellectual and knowledge oriented testing, the affective domain focuses on emotions and responses. Standardized tests in the affective domain can be used to compare the personality, traits, and interests of one client to a larger group as a whole (e.g., a test could be used to compare one student's interest level in math to another student's).

Some of the most common types of assessments used relating to the cognitive domain are attitude tests and personality tests. Counselors are able to use results from these tests to help clients because attitudes and personalities are key factors in how people lead their lives. By considering these factors when working with clients, counselors can be more effective.

Another way assessments can differ is if they require objective or subjective scoring and interpretation. Objective scoring means that an assessment does not require any personal interpretation. For example, generally with multiple choice tests or other cognitive-based assessments there is only one correct answer. Therefore, scoring the test simply requires marking the correct answers as correct and the incorrect answers as incorrect. Objectivity requires strict interpretations based on facts and figures, rather than any consideration of personal opinions, prejudices, or preconceived notions.

While there are a number of objective tests available in counseling, a large part of the counseling process instead involves subjective assessments and evaluations. Subjective tests either have multiple correct answers or no "correct" answer. They therefore require that the person administering them interpret the responses. Subjective tests can be given in a variety of formats, including short answer, essay, or face to face. Although most cognitive-based assessments are typically considered to be objective, there are situations in which they can be subjective as well. For example, a fill-in-the-blank assessment may have one correct answer, but multiple alternatives may be correct. The test would therefore require some subjective determinations be made by the scorer.

Both subjective and objective tests are useful in counseling. Objective tests are easier to administer to wide groups, and are generally less time and labor intensive to score and interpret. However, some information can only be gathered through subjective testing. Subjective tests can be more personalized, and allow direct considerations of factors such as language use, habits, or personality factors.

Regardless of the type of standardized test, two important elements to consider (which extend to any form of testing and assessment) are test reliability and test validity. **Test reliability** refers to the extent to which a test is consistent. Reliability is an important aspect of testing because if a test is not reliable then it is not comparable between individuals or different instances of testing. It may also not be a trustworthy measure of information.

An example of an **unreliable test** could be as simple as a broken bathroom scale. If a person stepped on a scale in the morning and it read 150 pounds, and later that same day they stepped on the scale and it read 250 pounds, they would most likely determine that the scale was unreliable. Similarly if a study is conducted which is meant to determine the extent to which an individual is affected by a phobia, and in one instance they score 90 percent and shortly afterwards they score 50 percent then the test is considered to be unreliable and cannot be trusted.

The second element, **test validity**, refers to the extent to which a test actually tests the information that it is meant to. Validity is the highest standard of testing and cannot be compromised under any circumstances. Validity is an important element of testing because if a test does not adequately fulfill its purpose than it may supply misleading or inadequate information. For example, if a test is designed to determine an individual's ability to perform complex calculus, but the questions all relate to basic addition, then the test would be invalid.

Another issue related to validity is the extent to which the tests can demonstrate true differences in individuals or circumstances. For example, if a test is meant to determine which applicant for a job is most knowledgeable about related subject matter. If two applicants take the tests, one who knows very little about the subject matter and one who is highly qualified, the test scores should reflect this (i.e., the two applicants should not receive similar scores).

Symptomatology is the study of symptoms that may indicate a disease. In the medical world symptomatology can be invaluable in helping doctors to narrow down the possibilities of illnesses that an individual may have, particularly because most symptoms are detectable only by the person experiencing them. Symptomatology also takes an important role in counseling because often psychological problems will begin to manifest themselves physically.

For example, excessive stress and depression can lead to weight fluctuations, headaches, and other problems. Furthermore, many psychological illnesses such as post-traumatic stress disorder or schizophrenia can only be identified by their symptoms – nightmares, hallucinations, etc. – because they do not manifest in any medically identifiable way.

Observation

Although testing is an important element of counseling and assessment, not all information can be gathered simply through testing clients. Rather, a primary way in which psychological information can be gathered is through the observation of subjects. Often, information can be gathered through observation that cannot be gathered through interviews or direct discussions with clients. For example, regardless of what a client is saying, aspects such as body language and other nonverbal indicators are extremely important to making correct interpretations. In this sense, observation is important when in direct contact with the client.

Observation is also often necessary on a wider scale as well. In some cases what the client says during sessions may not be entirely true. Not that this indicates that the client is being deceitful, but they may be interpreting situations incorrectly. Therefore, observations gathered either by the counselor themselves, or through seeking information from parents, siblings, teachers, co-workers, and others who observe them on a regular basis may be useful.

A variety of observation types exist. On the broadest level, observations can be classified as either direct or indirect. **Direct observation** involves the viewer (in most cases the counselor) actually being present to observe the situations. On the other hand, **indirect observation** describes situations in which case the person observing is not actually present. They therefore must gather the information indirectly, either through other people or through the use of technology such as cameras.

One type of direct observation is naturalistic observation. Naturalistic, or unobtrusive, observation describes observing subjects in their natural habitats; i.e., in normal situations. Naturalistic observation requires that the observer does not influence the subject's environment in any way, and for this reason it is also referred to as unobtrusive observation. The greatest benefit of naturalistic observation is that it allows the researcher to avoid any effects of the subject knowing they are being observed as this can often cause them to react differently to situations. It can therefore be valuable in determining actual responses to situations. Naturalistic observation can also be useful in allowing researchers to study situations which cannot be replicated in a lab, such as the effects of foster care or imprisonment.

However, one of the drawbacks of naturalistic observation is that there isn't a way to test specific situations. If the researcher wished to know how the person would react to failing a test, for example, they would have to hope that the situation arose naturally. Another difficulty with naturalistic observation is that isn't replicable and situations can't be repeated for further study and analysis.

Anecdotal records can be a form of indirect observation. Anecdotal records are written descriptions of everything that an observer sees. While the records need to be detailed enough to be useful, it is also important that they remain brief and focus on important events. An example of one type of anecdotal record is a student's permanent record. The permanent record holds information about the student's past class schedules, grades, and behaviors which can be useful in understanding their behaviors at present or future times.

Another observation method is frequency counting. **Frequency counting** is measuring the number of times that an event occurs. With this form of observation it is important that the most useful measures are selected to count. These measures will be unique to each client and their specific situations. They could be anything from counting the number of times that they make eye contact during a discussion, to the number of times that they talk with friends during a particular week.

A second important classification of observation methods is as structured or unstructured. Structured observation is essentially just what it sounds like. The observer will define ahead of time the elements and behaviors that they intend to observe, and will keep a careful record of them. Structured observation requires that the observer determine beforehand the behaviors of interest, the specific methods and types of measurement that will be used, and other aspects related to the observation. Because of this, structured observation is most useful when the counselor has a fair amount of control over the situation, and has already determined what behaviors are of interest in treating the patient. One of the greatest benefits of structured observation is that it allows the counselor to test or consider the impact of specific events or behaviors in the client's real-life context.

Unstructured observation, on the other hand, is not defined as specifically ahead of time as structured observation is. Rather, unstructured observation involves observing general situations and taking note of interesting or important occurrences. Whereas structured observation may look for specific behaviors as they occur in a variety of situations, unstructured observation involves looking at a variety of behaviors as they occur in a certain situation. Because of this, unstructured observations tend to be much more qualitative than structured observations, and allow counselors to gain information about a variety of behaviors.

The primary drawback of unstructured observation is that, by design, the most noticeable or conspicuous behaviors are recorded. However, it is not always the case that these are the most relevant behaviors to consider. By contrast, structured observation is careful to identify the most important behaviors to consider; however, as a result, it may cause any additional observations of important events to be overlooked as well. Often a mixing of structured and structured observations can be useful to avoid either problem from restricting the benefits of observation.

A third important classification of observation methods is as either participant or non-participant observations. Participant observations refer to situations in which the counselor becomes fully involved in the situation they are observing. This allows them to gather very useful data (both quantitative and qualitative) and to gain an integral understanding of the situations that their clients or subjects are in. However, some of the negatives of participant observations include the observer effect and the risk of subjectivity. The observer effect refers to the fact that if the subjects know that they are being observed by the counselor, they will alter their behavior accordingly. Subjectivity refers to the fact that the observations are subject to the counselor's interpretations of the situations, which may be limited or misconstrued. Both of these problems arise when the observation is overt, meaning that the subjects are aware of the counselor's role and purpose. On the other hand, covert observation is when the subjects are unaware of who the counselor really is. Subjectivity is also a risk factor in this type of situation, as is the problem of the counselor losing sight of their purpose if they become too immersed in the situation.

Non-participant observations are when the counselor observes the situations that the subjects are in, but does not actually participate in them personally. For example, often once during the year an administrator in a school situation will sit through a teacher's lessons. They are not involved in teaching, nor are they a student. Rather, they are non-participant observers. As with participant observation, non-participant observations can be either covert or overt. Overt non-participant observations tend to be easier and more straightforward; however, they also bring the risk (as with participant observations) of the observer effect. Covert non-participant observations do have an advantage over overt observations in the sense that they do not require the counselor to be able to integrate into the group; however, the observations may be less direct and accurate.

History of Assessments

The historical development of assessment and psychological testing has been a gradual process throughout the course of history. Although there were primitive counseling and testing practices as early as in ancient Greece or Rome, the real foundations of the testing movement can be traced to the development of the Simon-Binet scale at the beginning of the 1900s.

The scale was developed by Alfred Binet. Although he was originally trained as a lawyer, Binet's true interests always lay in psychology, and he was self-taught in the field. He began work on the scale when asked by the French government to develop a test that could be used in schools to determine which children should be placed in special classrooms for mental retardation. Essentially, the Binet-Simon scale was the first IQ test (although the term "IQ" was not applied to the test until later by a Stanford professor who modified it to result in a single quantitative output).

Binet developed the scale when he noticed, after testing the intelligence levels of many different children, that even at the same age, different children had different cognitive abilities. His test included considerations of various measures such as motor skills (such as shaking hands), to recall (such as the ability to repeat back a seven digit series of numbers), and language (such as the ability to form a sentence out of a set of random words). The test was designed to test the capabilities of children at different age levels, with the questioned being geared to the average capabilities of children of various ages.

Despite the importance of the development of the Binet-Simon scale, it has also received extensive criticism over time. Binet himself admitted that the test had many shortcomings; he believed that intelligence was really too vast a topic to be categorized into a single test or measurement. He believed that intelligence measures were diverse, and that they were highly influenced by environment. Because of this he stressed the importance of qualitative rather than quantitative measures. The scale is also often criticized because it cannot be standardized to a single test, but rather is composed of a series of 15 subtests which vary at different age levels.

However, despite the possible shortcomings of the scale, it quickly spread to the United States and became vastly popular. Various revised versions began to emerge, and intelligence tests were used widely during WWI to place recruits based on the assignments that they were most suited for and to select the most qualified recruits for leadership and other positions. Intelligence tests were also administered to immigrants and had influence over immigration policies and procedures.

After WWI, the popularity of testing in psychology-related fields continued to expand, and tests were developed for various uses such as determining interests, career development, and reasoning abilities. One of the most famous tests associated with the field of psychology is the Rorschach Inkblot Test. This test was devised in the early 1920s by Hermann Rorschach. His original use for it was as an attempt to create a test that could be used to profile schizophrenic patients. However, by the 1960s it had become one of the most popular methods of analyzing personality in general.

The Rorschach Inkblot Test consists of a series of ten inkblots which patients are asked to give an initial reaction to. Then, they are given a chance to more thoroughly examine the inkblots. The premise of the test is that how patients interpret the inkblots can give insight to their subconscious and personality. It is therefore especially useful with patients who either struggle with or are unwilling to share their thought patterns and processes. The biggest complaint about the test is that although there have been a few different attempts at creating a set scoring and analysis for patient responses, it is still fairly subjective because every patient responds uniquely to the test. Also, as a result of the fame of the test, information about the "correct" responses and resulting interpretations is readily available from many online sources, corrupting its use.

Another important test in the history of psychological testing is the Wechsler Adult Intelligence Scale (commonly abbreviated as WAIS). This test was developed by David Wechsler in the early 1940s. Much like Alfred Binet, Wechsler believed that intelligence should be classified less by an individual's straight cognitive abilities, and rather should be measured as a universal ability to reason logically, problem solve, and respond to their environment. As a result, he was frustrated by the limitations of the widely popular Binet scale (and its derivatives).

Wechsler's test, similar to Binet's, consisted of 10 different subtests in areas of verbal and performance based IQ. Scoring was based on an index similarly to the Simon-Binet scale, and has undergone many revisions with time. Wechsler himself expanded his test to apply separately to three different age ranges. The three tests are known as the Wechsler Intelligence Scale for Children (WISC), Wechsler Preschool and Primary Test for Intelligence (WPPTI), and the Wechsler Adult Intelligence Scale (WAIS).

As time progressed, however, there was increasing pressure for tests to be developed which were simpler, quicker, and more efficient to administer. One of the problems with all of the above tests is that they must be administered individually, and can be extremely time consuming (the original Simon-Binet test could last as long as three hours depending on the age, cooperation, and abilities of the subject). Increasing technology and the possibility of electronic scoring brought an increasingly varied range of tests and assessments over time.

DSM-IV

The real reason for various tests and assessments in counseling is to identify and classify various mental and psychological issues. While there is a great deal of controversy about the specifics of classifying diseases, the most widely accepted and referenced manual for classifying mental disorders is the Diagnostic and Statistical Manual of Mental Disorders, Fourth Edition, more commonly referred to as the DSM-IV. The

DSM-IV is an exhaustive compilation of information about many different levels and types of mental disorders. It includes information regarding definitions, symptoms, treatments, causes, and general statistics regarding all accepted mental disorders. The DSM-IV takes a multi-axial approach to defining the different disorders, with each of five different axes representing a different level of symptoms or difficulties that an individual may be struggling with.

The first axis, Axis I, describes the clinical symptoms of the individual. This is the immediate diagnosis that needs treating, and what people normally think of when they consider disorders. For example, schizophrenia, depression, anxiety disorders, bipolar disorder, and phobias are all classified under Axis I of the DSM-IV.

The second axis, Axis II, is reserved for developmental or personality disorders. The disorders classified on Axis II are typically long lasting, evident in childhood, and relate to how an individual interacts with the world around them. For example, mental retardation and various types of personality disorders are classified as Axis II disorders. Often Axis I disorders can be a direct result of Axis II disorders, such as if a patient with Antisocial Personality Disorder suffers recurring panic attacks, an Axis I disorder.

The third axis, Axis III, includes physical disorders or neurological problems which can result in or influence Axis I and II disorders. For example, an individual who suffers from diabetes may lead to fatigue which may lead to depression. Axis III disorders also include glaucoma, hypothyroidism, brain damage or diseases such as AIDS which lead to mental disorders. Simply put, Axis III disorders are physical problems affect an individual's psychological state.

Axis IV is used to classify social problems which have an influence on an individual's mental state. Major life changes or difficult situations are classified under Axis IV. For example, the death of a parent, child or other loved one, moving out for college, divorce, and unemployment could all be classified as an Axis IV problem. The problems classified under Axis IV are referred to as psychosocial problems.

The final axis, Axis V, is a rating which describes the patient's highest level of functioning. This rating plots an individual on a scale from 0 to 100 (with 100 indicating the highest level of functioning), and is often tracked over time to help in analyzing the effects of disorders over time.

 ## Sample Test Questions

1) The female psychoanalyst who rejected strict Freudian theory and posited that environmental and social conditions primarily determine individual personality and cause personality disorders more than instinctual or biological drives was

   A) Melanie Klein
   B) Anna Freud
   C) Karen Horney
   D) Mary Ainsworth

The correct answer is C:) Karen Horney.

2) Spirituality is

   A) Personal beliefs about intrinsic values and meanings in life
   B) The institutional setting of worship and dogmas or frameworks of morality
   C) Moral guidelines and value systems taught by churches by which individuals should live their lives
   D) None of the above

The correct answer is A:) Personal beliefs about intrinsic values and meanings in life. Answers B and C are more correctly descriptive of religion than spirituality.

3) The Civil Rights Act does NOT protect against discrimination based on

   A) Race
   B) Gender
   C) Sexual orientation
   D) Age

The correct answer is C:) Sexual orientation. However, there are laws which address discrimination based on sexual orientation in governmental settings.

4) What was the first major school of thought in psychology?

   A) Determinism
   B) Functionalism
   C) Structuralism
   D) Systems theory

The correct answer is C:) Structuralism. Structuralism did not last long as a theory because of its subjective and unreliable nature.

5) Which theory relied primarily on introspection for research?

   A) Logotherapy
   B) Structuralism
   C) Functionalism
   D) Factorism

The correct answer is B:) Structuralism. Subjects would consider their responses and try to deconstruct their reactions to the basic impulse behind them.

6) Which of the following is a teen most likely to consume?

   A) Cocaine
   B) Marijuana
   C) Alcohol
   D) Inhalants

The correct answer is C:) Alcohol. By a wide margin, alcohol is the most abused substance by teens.

7) The two most important developmental approaches in career development counseling are those of

   A) Ginzberg and Freud
   B) Super and Roe
   C) Roe and Freud
   D) Ginzberg and Super

The correct answer is D:) Ginzberg and Super. Freud is noted for developing the psychoanalytical perspective, and Roe's theories are of note in family counseling.

8) Which of the following individuals is associated with the founding of vocational counseling?

   A) Carl Rogers
   B) Frank Parsons
   C) Sigmund Freud
   D) Edward Titchener

The correct answer is B:) Frank Parsons. The origins of vocational counseling can be traced back to the work of Frank Parsons in the early 20th century.

9) Which of the following best summarizes the principles of Frank Parsons?

   A) If individuals are more satisfied and skilled in their work it will be better for the economy as a whole.
   B) Individuals need not specialize in any one area, rather scientific management should be used to standardize industries.
   C) It is more important that students study philosophy than train for future jobs because most work involves primarily on-the-job training.
   D) None of the above

The correct answer is A:) If individuals are more satisfied and skilled in their work it will be better for the economy as a whole. He encouraged workers to consider what their skills were, and what type of work would make them happy.

10) Which of the following is NOT an element of nonverbal communication?

   A) Posture
   B) Eye movement
   C) Paralanguage
   D) All of the above are elements of nonverbal communication

The correct answer is C:) Paralanguage. Paralanguage refers to elements within verbalized communication such as tone, pitch, tempo, and volume which enhance communication.

11) According to Erikson's developmental stages, what important event accompanies initiative vs. guilt conflict?

   A) Work and parenthood
   B) Exploration
   C) School
   D) Toilet training

The correct answer is B:) Exploration. During this stage, children begin asserting control over the environment.

12) In which of the following situations would a counselor NOT be ethically justified in breaking confidentiality?

   A) When the client is determined to be a danger to themselves.
   B) If the client has seriously threatened the counselor's life.
   C) When the counselor becomes aware of ongoing child abuse.
   D) If the client is cheating on their spouse.

The correct answer is D:) If the client is cheating on their spouse. The counselor would not be allowed to break confidentiality in this situation; however, they would in each of the preceding three.

13) Counselors should NOT cultivate tendencies to

   A) Focus on the needs of the client
   B) Tell personal stories often
   C) Balance consistency and flexibility
   D) Be non-judgmental of past mistakes

The correct answer is B:) Tell personal stories often. While communication and familiarity are important between a counselor and client, the focus of counseling should be on the client, not the counselor.

14) Which of the following is a basic assumption of psychodynamic therapy?

   A) All individuals will react essentially the same to different situations.
   B) Actions are largely controlled by unconscious motivations.
   C) People are naturally honest, good, and capable of progression.
   D) An individual's actions are largely controlled by their conscious thought.

The correct answer is B:) Actions are largely controlled by unconscious motivations. This is one way in which psychodynamic therapy and psychotherapy are similar.

15) The act which is designed to ensure that people with disabilities receive the same opportunities as those without disabilities is the

   A) Disabled Americans Act
   B) Americans with Disabilities Act
   C) Protective Act for the Severely Disabled
   D) Equal Opportunity Act

The correct answer is B:) Americans with Disabilities Act. The ADA applies to all governmental programs and to private employers with more than 15 employees.

16) A holistic approach to treating disorders takes into account

   A) Mental factors
   B) Social factors
   C) Physical symptoms
   D) All of the above

The correct answer is D:) All of the above.

17) Typically, girls tend to excel in school if they can

   A) Relate things to their own lives or the real world
   B) Consider things analytically or mechanically
   C) See a mathematical justification for things
   D) Both B and C

The correct answer is A:) Relate things to their own lives or the real world. By contrast, boys tend to be more analytical and mechanical in their approach.

18) Which of the following is a technique for overcoming phobias?

   A) DSM-IV
   B) Trait-factor analysis
   C) Naturalistic observation
   D) Systematic desensitization

The correct answer is D:) Systematic desensitization. This is essentially a process of vivid imagination through which a person acclimatizes themselves to their phobia.

19) Initially, the counseling profession was applied to which field?

   A) Treatment of mental health patients
   B) Vocational development
   C) Learning disorders
   D) None of the above

The correct answer is B:) Vocational development. The field developed largely due to the efforts and principles of Frank Parsons.

20) The origins of deinstitutionalization are associated with which time period?

   A) 1600s
   B) 1700s
   C) 1800s
   D) 1900s

The correct answer is D:) 1900s. The deinstitutionalization movement began in the twentieth century as a result of the declining state of mental care facilities.

21) It is better to take counseling as a child than as an adult because

   A) Children's minds are more impressionable
   B) Childhood problems tend to have a significant impact on future life
   C) It is easier to identify the root of a problem when a patient is younger
   D) All of the above

The correct answer is D:) All of the above. These are a few of the reasons why it is considered easier to take counseling as a child than an adult.

22) Systematic desensitization works based on the principle of

   A) Trait-factor analysis
   B) Unobtrusive observation
   C) Classical conditioning
   D) Qualia

The correct answer is C:) Classical conditioning. The idea is that when transferring from imagined situations to actual situations, classical conditioning will allow the same, calm responses.

23) Albert Bandura is associated with

   A) Family systems therapy
   B) Structuralism
   C) Social learning theory
   D) Gestalt therapy

The correct answer is C:) Social learning theory. Bandura believed that traditional instruction and reinforcement patterns were not the only way that people learned, and that observation is key.

24) Which of the following was most important in perpetuating the deinstitutionalization movement?

   A) The increase in funding for mental care facilities.
   B) The development of psychiatric medicine.
   C) The ineffectiveness of mental care facilities.
   D) The temporary nature of most mental health problems.

The correct answer is B:) The development of psychiatric medicine. This along with the consistent underfunding and overcrowding of mental care facilities spurred the movement.

25) In situations where ethics are in question, a counselor should remember that their first duty is to

   A) Their practice
   B) The government
   C) The patient's family
   D) The patient

The correct answer is D:) The patient. A counselor must to work to maintain their confidentiality, ensure informed consent, and be sure that their own biases are not affecting their treatment of the patient.

26) Ann Roe identified three different parent-child relationships which she correlated to their needs later in life. According to Roe, a child in a situation of "avoidance of the child" would seek fulfillment of

   A) Lower-level needs relating to material considerations
   B) Mid-level needs relating to emotional fulfillment
   C) High-level needs relating to fulfillment and achievement
   D) Lower-level needs relating to emotional fulfillment

The correct answer is A:) Lower-level needs relating to material considerations. Children in a state of "concentration on the child" seek mid-level needs, and those in "acceptance of the child" seek high-level.

27) Because they tend to shy away from the concept of mental disturbance, Asian patients often present more

   A) Emotional symptoms
   B) Somatic symptoms
   C) Psychological symptoms
   D) None of the above

The correct answer is B:) Somatic symptoms. They tend to accept treatment of physical problems above those involving mental or emotional issues.

28) One of the largest problems contributing to lower use of counseling services among minority groups is the

   A) Unavailability of counselors of different races
   B) Inability of potential clients to access counseling services
   C) Rampant discrimination at the hands of counselors
   D) None of the above

The correct answer is A:) Unavailability of counselors of different races. Most individuals feel more comfortable going to a counselor of their same race; however, counselors continue to be predominantly white.

29) In order to resolve the Oedipus complex, a child must

   A) Identify with the same-sex parent
   B) Identify with the opposite-sex parent
   C) Form the super-ego
   D) Repress the feelings

The correct answer is A:) Identify with the same-sex parent. A boy must resolve the conflict he feels with his father by identifying with him to overcome the Oedipus complex.

30) DSM-IV codes are set up as classifications of disorders based on

   A) The severity of the disorder
   B) The causes of the disorder
   C) The treatment of the disorder
   D) The specific nature of the disorder

The correct answer is D:) The specific nature of the disorder.

31) Attempting to increase the value of the nurturing role of women is most consistent with which feminist model?

   A) Liberal
   B) Social
   C) Radical
   D) Cultural

The correct answer is D:) Cultural. The cultural model is essentially opposite of the liberal model which stresses the importance of decreasing barriers to equality.

32) Which of the following correctly lists the six personality types identified by Holland?

   A) Realistic, investigative, artistic, social, enterprising, and conventional
   B) Realistic, emotional, technical, artistic, investigative, and social
   C) Emotional, artistic, social, conventional, realistic, and enterprising
   D) Technical, emotional, actualizing, social, investigative, and conventional

The correct answer is A:) Realistic, investigative, artistic, social, enterprising, and conventional. These traits can be remembered using the RIASEC acronym.

33) If a person needed help determining which career path they were best suited for, they would most likely seek

   A) Adlerian counseling
   B) Career counseling
   C) Cognitive therapy
   D) Systems therapy

The correct answer is B:) Career counseling. The field of career counseling has the specific focus of helping individuals with their career options.

34) Erik Erikson's theory of psychosocial development demonstrates the impact of _____ on human development.

   A) Behavior
   B) Biological predispositions
   C) Social experience
   D) All of the above

The correct answer is C:) Social experience. The word "psychosocial" combines the words psychological (mind) and social (relationships).

35) Karen Horney believed that people with minor neurotic problems

   A) Probably suffered from neglect
   B) Don't really have neurosis
   C) Can treat themselves
   D) Two of the above

The correct answer is C:) Can treat themselves. Horney often encouraged self-analysis and self-help. She believed that, regarding relatively minor neurotic problems, people could be their own psychiatrists.

36) In many cases it is easier to take counseling as

   A) An adult than as a child
   B) A boss than as an employee
   C) A child than as an adult
   D) None of the above

The correct answer is C:) A child than as an adult. One of the most important reasons for this is that children tend to be more impressionable, and it is more difficult to change as an adult.

37) Which of the following statements is FALSE?

   A) Differences between learning styles of genders is typically more pronounced as they age.
   B) Gender differences in learning styles are likely a result of cultural norms and genetic or neurological factors.
   C) Both of the above statements are false.
   D) All of the above statements are true.

The correct answer is A:) Differences between learning styles of genders is typically more pronounced as they age. Differences in gender learning styles tend to lessen with age (i.e., the differences are much less exaggerated in a high school classroom than a kindergarten classroom).

38) According to Freud's personality theory, which of the following is present at birth?

   A) Id
   B) Ego
   C) Superego
   D) Id and ego

The correct answer is A:) Id.

39) Which of the following is NOT a step in the assessment process?

   A) Identify the purpose of counseling
   B) Clarify the situation
   C) Determine how to proceed with counseling
   D) Administer a battery of long and thorough tests

The correct answer is D:) Administer a battery of long and thorough tests. Answers A, B, and C correctly identify the first three steps of the assessment process. The fourth is to implement the procedures determined in the third step.

40) If a therapist were to treat a close friend it would be referred to as a(n)

   A) Dual relationship
   B) Unethical interaction
   C) Objectivity barrier
   D) Behavior of questionable practicality

The correct answer is A:) Dual relationship. Dual relationships can occur in many different situations, such as if a therapist is also a friend to, a family member of, sexually involved with, or a business partner of a person that they are treating.

41) A counselor wishing to direct the flow of conversation would use

   A) Three-pronged appraisal techniques
   B) Close-ended questions
   C) Open-ended questions
   D) Aptitude tests

The correct answer is B:) Close-ended questions. Close-ended questions are appropriate when a counselor wants to illicit decisiveness, or simply wants a specific question added.

42) Neurotics who do not have their needs met will experience high levels of

    A) Depression
    B) Stress
    C) Anxiety
    D) All of the above

The correct answer is C:) Anxiety. Psychologist Karen Horney explained that while neuroticism is felt by everybody to some extent, a neurotic's needs are much more intense, to the point they will experience great anxiety if their needs is not met.

43) Which of the following IS an example of intentional body language?

    A) Paralanguage
    B) Unconscious expression
    C) Affect-display actions
    D) None of the above

The correct answer is C:) Affect-display actions. Affect-display actions are commonly used, intentional actions (including facial expressions and gestures) which are used to convey emotions.

44) According to Abraham Maslow, when self-actualization needs are not met, people

    A) Become neurotic
    B) Are motivated by deficiency needs
    C) Suffer from metapathology
    D) Are motivated by esteem needs

The correct answer is C:) Suffer from metapathology. Metapathology occurs when an individual's metaneeds are not satisfied.

45) Which of the following is NOT a "deficiency need?"

    A) Social needs
    B) Safety needs
    C) Esteem needs
    D) None of the above

The correct answer is D:) None of the above. Physiological, security, social, and esteem needs are "deficiency needs" which arise from deprivation.

46) A patient suffering from depression feels as though their life has no purpose, and that they cannot make it have purpose. Their therapist focuses their attention on finding the meaning of their life, and convincing them that no matter what, all life has meaning. This approach is most correctly described as

   A) Gestalt therapy
   B) Holistic therapy
   C) Logotherapy
   D) Cognitive therapy

The correct answer is C:) Logotherapy. Logotherapy is based off the belief that all life has meaning, people have a will to meaning and that people can harness it to pursue a better life.

47) Binet and Wechsler both felt that intelligence

   A) Could be easily quantified based on a single cognitive test.
   B) Involves a much wider scale of considerations than straight cognitive abilities.
   C) Cannot be quantified by any method, and it should not be attempted.
   D) Is only measurable at a very early age.

The correct answer is B:) Involves a much wider scale of considerations than straight cognitive abilities. Each developed an intelligence test based on this belief.

48) A therapist notes that their client who has diabetes suffers from chronic depression. Which of these problems would be classified on Axis I of the DSM-IV?

   A) Depression
   B) Diabetes
   C) Both
   D) Neither

The correct answer is A:) Depression. Axis I relates to the clinical symptoms, in this case depression. These can be caused by physical disorders, such as diabetes, which are classified on Axis III.

49) _____ is the ethical component of personality and provides moral standards.

   A) Id
   B) Ego
   C) Superego
   D) Id and ego

The correct answer is C:) Superego.

50) The theory of the collective unconscious is associated with which branch of theory?

   A) Analytical perspective
   B) Psychodynamic theory
   C) Adlerian theory
   D) Logotherapy

The correct answer is A:) Analytical perspective. The analytical perspective was developed by Carl Jung. He believed that people were influenced by their personal experiences and the shared experience of human understanding.

51) Which of the following is a basic assumption of person-centered therapy?

   A) All healthy individuals will react essentially the same to different situations.
   B) Actions are largely controlled by unconscious motivations.
   C) People are naturally honest, good, and capable of progression.
   D) An individual's actions are entirely controlled by their conscious thoughts and decisions.

The correct answer is C:) People are naturally honest, good, and capable of progression. In this way, person-centered therapy is humanistic in its approach.

52) Axis IV of the DSM-IV is used to classify

   A) Clinical symptoms
   B) Personality disorders
   C) Physical disorders
   D) Social problems

The correct answer is D:) Social problems. For example, major life changes such as the death of a relative would be classified on Axis IV.

53) Which of the following is NOT a model to describe perceptions about disability?

   A) Moral
   B) Medical
   C) Mistake
   D) Minority

The correct answer is C:) Mistake. The three models used to describe perceptions about disabilities are the moral model, the medical model, and the minority model.

54) According to Maslow's theory, which of the following is TRUE?

   A) A person must feel safe to be concerned about hunger.
   B) A person must feel loved to feel safe and secure.
   C) A person must feel safe to have self-esteem.
   D) A person must achieve self-actualization to have self-esteem.

The correct answer is C:) A person must feel safe to have self-esteem. Esteem is higher up in Maslow's hierarchy of needs than is safety.

55) Which of the following became famous for his experiments with dogs and conditioning?

   A) Alfred Kinsey
   B) Carl Jung
   C) B. F. Skinner
   D) Ivan Pavlov

The correct answer is D:) Ivan Pavlov.

56) In the early 1920s Hermann Rorschach developed a test involving the use of

   A) Cards with inkblots on them
   B) A series of standardized questions about hobbies and interests
   C) Quizzes to test analytical tendencies
   D) Interpersonal skill ratings

The correct answer is A:) Cards with inkblots on them. A patient's response to the cards was seen as an indicator of personality.

57) Which of the following is NOT true regarding NBCC certification?

   A) Attaining NBCC certification requires graduation from an accredited university.
   B) NCC certification requires an applicant to pass the NCE – National Counselor Exam.
   C) The NBCC was created by the APA.
   D) The certification offered by the NBCC is referred to as the NCC – National Counselor Certification.

The correct answer is C:) The NBCC was created by the APA. The NBCC was created by the ACA.

58) The main purpose of AA is to

   A) Research alcoholism
   B) Implement the 12 steps
   C) Help alcoholics get sober
   D) None of the above

The correct answer is C:) Help alcoholics get sober. AA (Alcoholics Anonymous) is an organization that helps alcoholics achieve and maintain sobriety.

59) Family counseling can best be described as

   A) Analyzing how a person's family interactions may be causing their internal struggles.
   B) Asking a person about their feelings regarding their relationship with their parents.
   C) Involving entire families in the counseling process and treating them as a cohesive unit.
   D) None of the above

The correct answer is C:) Involving entire families in the counseling process and treating them as a cohesive unit. The primary objective of the therapist in family therapy is to understand the interactions that occur between people, rather than analyzing the actions or conflicts within a specific individual.

60) Understanding the interactions between family members is an important aspect of

   A) Family systems therapy
   B) Holistic therapy
   C) Multicultural therapy
   D) Interrelatedness therapy

The correct answer is A:) Family systems therapy. The primary focus of family therapy is to improve relations within a family.

61) According to instinct theory, human behavior is driven by

   A) Survival
   B) Learned behaviors
   C) Biological instincts
   D) Genetic disposition

The correct answer is C:) Biological instincts. Instinct theory says that all organisms are born with genetically programmed tendencies that drive their behavior.

62) Which of the following is NOT an important area of study in Adlerian philosophy?

   A) Work
   B) Social and family
   C) Love and sexuality
   D) Relaxation and friendship

The correct answer is D:) Relaxation and friendship. Answers A, B, and C are the three areas of conflict which Adler believed a person experienced.

63) That changing thought processes will result in improved behavior is an important assumption of

   A) Eclecticism
   B) Cognitive-behavioral therapies
   C) Holistic therapy
   D) All of the above

The correct answer is B:) Cognitive-behavioral therapies.

64) Although a test gives consistent scoring, two individuals with extremely different levels of qualification both receive similar scores. This describes a problem with

   A) Test reliability
   B) Test understandability
   C) Test comprehension
   D) Test validity

The correct answer is D:) Test validity. Test validity also describes situations in which the test does not adequately test the information that it is meant to.

65) A researcher counts the number of times during a session that a client mentions their family. This is an example of which observation method?

   A) Unstructured
   B) Frequency counting
   C) Tallying
   D) Anecdotal record

The correct answer is B:) Frequency counting. This could also be called a type of structured observation (not unstructured).

66) Which is NOT one of the three main coping strategies in Karen Horney's ten neurosis?

   A) Withdrawal
   B) Acting out
   C) Aggression
   D) Compliance

The correct answer is B:) Acting out. Horney identified three main coping strategies within the ten neuroses: compliance (moving towards others) aggression (moving against others) and withdrawal (moving away from others).

67) The basic assumption of holistic therapy is that

   A) A person's mental, physical, and spiritual health are all connected.
   B) People are victims of circumstance.
   C) The main drive of an individual is finding meaning in life.
   D) Actions are a result of thought processes.

The correct answer is A:) A person's mental, physical, and spiritual health are all connected. Holistic therapy considers individuals in terms of overall health.

68) Which of the following classifications involves the culture a person lives in?

   A) Nationality
   B) Race
   C) Ethnicity
   D) Lineage

The correct answer is C:) Ethnicity. Nationality is a classification by citizenship, and race is a classification based on biological factors.

69) The approach in counseling which considers the cultural factors relevant to a specific client is

   A) Multicultural therapy
   B) Systems therapy
   C) Culture-bias therapy
   D) Eclectic therapy

The correct answer is A:) Multicultural therapy. Culture is an essential part of who a person is, and multicultural therapy recognizes this fact.

70) A client of Hispanic descent would most characteristically prefer which type of therapy?

   A) Gestalt therapy
   B) Individual therapy
   C) Phenomenological therapy
   D) Family therapy

The correct answer is D:) Family therapy. The responsibility of family in supporting one another is taken very seriously, and obligations between family members are strong.

71) In Gestalt therapy, what constitutes unfinished business?

   A) Tasks which clients have always wished to complete but never have.
   B) Relationships which clients are sorry to have seen end and wish to renew.
   C) Conflicts which have remained unresolved and are affecting the client's daily functioning.
   D) None of the above

The correct answer is C:) Conflicts which have remained unresolved and are affecting the client's daily functioning. In Gestalt therapy, resolving unfinished business is considered important to increasing self-awareness and happiness.

72) In cognitive therapy, mental filter describes situations in which an individual

    A) Sees things in terms of how they think they should be, and not how they actually are.
    B) Treats positive situations as though they are less relevant than negative situations.
    C) Has a tendency to see only the negative aspects of a situation.
    D) Assumes that because something happened once, it must be true in all situations.

The correct answer is C:) Has a tendency to see only the negative aspects of a situation. Mental filter is an example of a faulty thought process which can lead to depression in cognitive theory.

73) The goal in psychodynamic therapy is to

    A) Show the client that there is always a meaning in life.
    B) Identify and work through events resulting in maladaptive functions of the subconscious.
    C) Classify the client's thought processes to better understand the inner workings of the brain.
    D) None of the above

The correct answer is B:) Identify and work through events resulting in maladaptive functions of the subconscious. A psychodynamic therapist will work to build a relationship with a client, and then help them in confronting their problems.

74) The approach of considering individuals in the context of the people and social structures around them is referred to as

    A) Logotherapy
    B) Systematic desensitization
    C) Social learning theory
    D) Systems therapy

The correct answer is D:) Systems therapy. Systems therapy resists the notion that individuals can be understood by studying the minute details at work within them (as psychoanalysis suggests).

75) The concept of dynamic equilibrium in systems therapy refers to

   A) The fact that while the balance of the system is maintained, individual relationships are constantly changing.
   B) A state in which individual relationships remain at a static balance, whereas overall equilibrium shifts.
   C) Environments in which a high premium is placed on the ability to maintain a status quo.
   D) None of the above

The correct answer is A:) The fact that while the balance of the system is maintained, individual relationships are constantly changing. Dynamic equilibrium is an important concept in systems therapy.

76) Although one individual will benefit most from group counseling, it would be detrimental to an individual who needs the attention of individual counseling. This demonstrates the need for which type of approach?

   A) Eclectic
   B) Gestalt
   C) Holistic
   D) Psychodynamic

The correct answer is A:) Eclectic. Eclecticism is characterized by combining a number of different approaches in treatment. This ensures that the client's needs are best met.

77) Counselors must be comfortable addressing matters relating to _____ with their clients.

   A) AIDS
   B) Disability
   C) Gender
   D) All of the above

The correct answer is D:) All of the above. Counselors face a wide variety of client situations and must be comfortable in discussing them.

78) The concept of career maturity was set forth by

   A) Super
   B) Ginzberg
   C) Holland
   D) Roe

The correct answer is A:) Super. Super defined career maturity as a measure of the extent to which a person has progressed through the career development process.

79) An individual's beliefs about their own capabilities and preferences, in combination with self-esteem and perceived needs, constitutes

   A) Self-image
   B) Career maturity
   C) Vocational self-concept
   D) Life stage development

The correct answer is C:) Vocational self-concept. Super considered vocational self-concept is an important element of career development.

80) How should counselors respond to questions of religion?

   A) Religion is always a positive influence, and counselors should always advise clients to attend church.
   B) Because religious observance can have negative impacts, counselors should avoid the topic.
   C) In terms of client spirituality, a counselor should consider each case individually.
   D) None of the above

The correct answer is C:) In terms of client spirituality, a counselor should consider each case individually. Because every situation is different it is important that counselor considers the details of each case to decide what the appropriate action is.

81) Which of the following does NOT describe a benefit to drug abusers of group therapy?

   A) It gives them an opportunity to learn from people who have progressed farther than they have.
   B) It gives them a support group that has a personal understanding of their struggles.
   C) It provides an open setting in which they can discuss their frustrations freely with others.
   D) All of the above are benefits of group therapy.

The correct answer is D:) All of the above are benefits of group therapy.

82) The list of tasks which a person is responsible to perform is their

   A) Occupation
   B) Job
   C) Career
   D) Obligation

The correct answer is B:) Job. For example, it may be a person's job to clean up tables after people eat, or to teach students about biology.

83) Which of the following is NOT an assumption of social learning theory?

   A) People can learn through observation
   B) Things that people observe are always reflected in their actions
   C) Intrinsic motivations are important in the learning process
   D) Learning can come from observing directly, through media, or through descriptions

The correct answer is B:) Things that people observe are always reflected in their actions. The theory states that there are many factors which influence whether or not a person demonstrates the traits that were learned.

84) Which of the following correctly lists the levels of Maslow's hierarchy of needs from lowest to highest?

   A) Safety, esteem, physiological, love and belonging, self-actualization
   B) Self-actualization, esteem, safety, love and belonging, physiological
   C) Physiological, safety, love and belonging, esteem, self-actualization
   D) Safety, physiological, love and belonging, esteem, self-actualization

The correct answer is C:) Physiological, safety, love and belonging, esteem, self-actualization. Answer D is the second closest answer, however it swaps the first two levels.

85) Psychologist William McDougall defined an instinct in three ways. Which of the following is NOT one of the three ways McDougall defined an instinct?

   A) Universal in a species
   B) Uniform in expression
   C) Unlearned
   D) Genetically programmed

The correct answer is D:) Genetically programmed. McDougall defined an instinct as a behavior that is A) unlearned, B) uniform in expression, and C) universal in a species.

86) The pathway which an individual takes relating to work throughout their life is their

   A) Career
   B) Job
   C) Occupation
   D) Profession

The correct answer is A:) Career. Career development is the process of career education, decision making, and career guidance throughout a person's life.

87) One of the most common applications of the trait and factor theory is in the field of

   A) Psychiatry
   B) Criminology
   C) Career counseling
   D) Study of mental disorders

The correct answer is C:) Career counseling. For example, aptitude tests are used to determine the traits which a person possesses, and they are then matched with a compatible job field.

88) An aptitude test may be used to

   A) Screen employees for job positions
   B) Test the fitness of an individual
   C) Help determine what jobs would be best for a person
   D) Both A and C

The correct answer is D:) Both A and C. They can be based on anything from numeric abilities, abstract reasoning, mechanical knowledge or any other information considered important to the employer.

89) A family moves to the United States from Mexico. With time, they begin to take on elements of American culture; however, they strive to retain some elements of their Mexican culture as well. This describes

   A) Assimilation
   B) Cultural pluralism
   C) Acculturation
   D) Racial discrimination

The correct answer is C:) Acculturation. Assimilation, on the other hand, would involve the initial culture being supplanted by the new culture.

90) According to Erikson's developmental stages, what basic conflict is associated with the early childhood stage?

   A) Autonomy vs. Shame and Doubt
   B) Trust vs. Mistrust
   C) Initiative vs. Guilt
   D) Industry vs. Interiority

The correct answer is A:) Autonomy vs. Shame and Doubt. During early childhood, children experience the autonomy vs. shame and doubt conflict while they potty train.

91) A person who views their own culture as superior to all others is said to be

   A) Acculturated
   B) Egocentric
   C) Stereotypical
   D) Ethnocentric

The correct answer is D:) Ethnocentric. A person with an ethnocentric mindset will often view their own culture as dominant and then rank all others in relation to it. Ethnocentricity will often lead to stereotyping and racism.

92) Which of the following does NOT describe a problem of test validity?

   A) It does not adequately demonstrate differences between individuals or circumstances.
   B) It does not give a consistent or standard score between individuals or different takings.
   C) It does not accurately test the information that it is meant to.
   D) All of the above describe problems with test validity.

The correct answer is B:) It does not give a consistent or standard score between individuals or different takings. This describes a problem of test reliability, not test validity.

93) Eating or sleep disorders are classified in which axis of the DSM-IV?

   A) Axis I
   B) Axis II
   C) Axis III
   D) Axis IV

The correct answer is A:) Axis I. Axis I includes clinical disorders usually diagnosed in infancy, childhood, or adolescence.

94) According to Karen Horney, neurosis is

   A) A coping technique
   B) Caused by abuse and neglect in childhood
   C) An uncommon occurrence
   D) All of the above

The correct answer is A:) A coping technique. Horney saw neurosis as an attempt to make life bearable.

95) Which of the following terms are synonymous?

   Naturalistic observation
   Unobtrusive observation
   Subjective observation

   A) I and II
   B) II and III
   C) I, II and III
   D) None of the terms are synonymous

The correct answer is A:) I and II. Naturalistic and unobtrusive observation are interchangeable terms referring to observing a subject in their natural habitat.

96) Which of the following individuals would NOT be helped through career counseling?

   A) An individual who has difficulty keeping a job.
   B) An individual who feels stagnant and unfulfilled in their work.
   C) An individual who is planning their future career path.
   D) All of the above could be helped by career counseling.

The correct answer is D:) All of the above could be helped by career counseling. A person would typically go to a career counselor if they are considering changing jobs, having difficulties holding jobs, having difficulties finding a job that suits them, or simply planning for the future.

97) A career counselor should focus on helping their clients

   A) Find satisfaction with the job they are currently in.
   B) Increase education to transition to a higher paying job.
   C) Explore many different career possibilities.
   D) Blindly chose a specific career and move towards it.

The correct answer is C:) Explore many different career possibilities. This way the client can become more attuned to their own preferences and strengths.

98) The Rorschach Inkblot Test is used in analyzing

   A) Physical disabilities
   B) Anger management capability
   C) Mental disorder
   D) Personality

The correct answer is D:) Personality. Initially it was developed to identify individuals with schizophrenia based on personality characteristics.

99) Who is known as the founder of gender difference psychology?

   A) Karen Horney
   B) Melanie Klein
   C) Anna Freud
   D) Carol Gilligan

The correct answer is D:) Carol Gilligan. Gender difference psychology focuses on the differences between how men and women think. According to Gilligan, these differences arise from social influences and gender conditioning.

100) The Oedipus complex occurs during which of Freud's stages of psychosexual development?

   A) Oral
   B) Anal
   C) Phallic
   D) Genital

The correct answer is C:) Phallic. The Oedipus complex is the son's desire for his mother and conflict with his father experienced in the phallic stage of psychosexual development.

101) Methods which focus on the process of unlearning negative behaviors and thought processes and learning positive behaviors are referred to as

   A) Logotherapeutic
   B) Gestaltic
   C) Freudian
   D) Cognitive-behavioral

The correct answer is D:) Cognitive-behavioral. Cognitive-behavioral methods focus on the relationship between thought processes and behavior.

102) Aaron T. Beck is associated with which of the following therapies?

   A) Behavioral therapy
   B) Social therapy
   C) Vocational therapy
   D) Cognitive therapy

The correct answer is D:) Cognitive therapy. Cognitive therapy is a theory which was developed by psychiatrist Aaron T. Beck, and it falls under the larger branch of cognitive-behavioral therapies.

103) Which of the following is NOT one of Karen Horney's ten identified neuroses?

   A) The need for power
   B) The need for simplicity
   C) The need for belonging
   D) The need for personal accomplishment

The correct answer is C:) The need for belonging. Horney described ten neuroses, including 1) the need for acceptance and affection, 2) love and intimacy, 3) simplicity, 4) power, 5) the need to manipulate, 6) social recognition, 7) admiration, 8) personal accomplishment, 9) independence, and 10) perfection.

104) When working with minority groups, it is best for counselors to have

   A) Indirect education about the culture
   B) Direct experience with the culture
   C) Empathy for the pressure to assimilate
   D) Understanding of common stereotypes

The correct answer is B:) Direct experience with the culture. This is especially true when counselors are working with younger clients.

105) If a counselor is working with a Hispanic family, it is important to understand cultural factors – such as the traditional masculine role of fathers referred to as

   A) Marianismo
   B) El fuerto
   C) Machismo
   D) Familism

The correct answer is C:) Machismo. The feminine role of the mothers is marianismo.

106) A person has an accident resulting in permanent brain damage. The brain damage results in a certain personality disorder and as a result the person has anxiety attacks in public situations. The proper classification of these problems under DSM-IV is

A) Brain damage: Axis III, personality disorder: Axis II, anxiety attacks: Axis I
B) Brain damage: Axis II, personality disorder and anxiety attacks: Axis I
C) Brain damage: Axis I, personality disorder: Axis II, anxiety attacks: Axis III
D) Brain damage: Axis III, personality disorder: Axis I, anxiety attacks: Axis II

The correct answer is A:) Brain damage: Axis III, personality disorder: Axis II, anxiety attacks: Axis I. Axis I is clinical symptoms, Axis II is personality disorders and developmental problems, and Axis III is physical disorders or problems.

107) In career counseling an individual may be asked to take a test to determine which jobs are most compatible with their personality type. This is referred to as a(n)

A) Cognitive abilities test
B) Vocational test
C) Logic test
D) Aptitude test

The correct answer is D:) Aptitude test. In the field of career counseling aptitude tests are often used to gather information about a person and what their interests or skills are.

108) A therapist uses both cognitive theory and holistic therapy in treating a patient. This would be described as

A) Gestalt therapy
B) Eclecticism
C) Logotherapy
D) Deinstitutionalization

The correct answer is B:) Eclecticism. Eclecticism is characterized by combining a number of different approaches in treatment.

109) Which of the following BEST describes the deinstitutionalization movement?

A) A movement towards placing patients in long-term, stated-owned facilities.
B) A movement towards putting patients through short-term holistic counseling.
C) A movement towards placing patients in localized community facilities offering outpatient care.
D) None of the above

The correct answer is C:) A movement towards placing patients in localized community facilities offering outpatient care. This was a result of the under-funding of programs, inadequacy of care, and the development of psychiatric medicine which made perpetual treatment unnecessary for some patients.

110) Dorothea Dix is associated with the development of which of the following?

A) Treatment of mentally ill individuals
B) Treatment of depressed and suicidal patients
C) Vocational therapy
D) Psychoanalytical psychology

The correct answer is A:) Treatment of mentally ill individuals. At the time, the treatment of the mentally ill was poor and inhumane. Dix devoted her life to improving treatment of mentally ill individuals.

111) Karen Horney believed that _____ in childhood is the cause of neurosis in adults.

A) Parental indifference
B) Neglect
C) Abuse
D) Abnormal development

The correct answer is A:) Parental indifference. Horney called parental indifference the "basic evil."

112) Which field of counseling is unique in its focus on interpersonal relations and the interactions of members of a group?

   A) Marriage and family counseling
   B) Therapeutic counseling
   C) Rehabilitation counseling
   D) Mental health counseling

The correct answer is A:) Marriage and family counseling. Rehabilitation counseling, mental health counseling, and therapeutic counseling are all individual-based forms of counseling.

113) In Gestalt therapy, the most important aspect is

   A) The past
   B) The present
   C) The future
   D) A combination of past and future

The correct answer is B:) The present. Gestalt therapy is existential in this sense because it focuses on current actions and interdependence.

114) A therapist is working with an individual who, although they often score very well on their tests, treats these accomplishments as irrelevant and feels as though they always do poorly. The therapist would describe their mindset as

   A) Mental filter
   B) Disqualifying the positive
   C) Should rationalization
   D) Overgeneralization

The correct answer is B:) Disqualifying the positive. Disqualifying the positive is when the patient's view of positive things as being irrelevant or less important than the negative things.

115) Albert Ellis is associated with which theory?

   A) Rational emotive behavior therapy
   B) Psychodynamic
   C) Logotherapy
   D) Structuralism

The correct answer is A:) Rational emotive behavior therapy. Ellis developed REBT in the 1950s.

116) What federal organization provides occupational information?

   A) Department of Agriculture
   B) Department of Labor
   C) Department of State
   D) Department of Commerce

The correct answer is D:) Department of Commerce. The U.S. Department of Commerce promotes job creation, economic growth, sustainable development and improved standards of living for Americans.

117) Of the following individuals, who is most associated with logotherapy?

   A) Victor Frankel
   B) Dr. Kavorkian
   C) Carl Rogers
   D) Edmund Husserl

The correct answer is A:) Victor Frankel. Frankel argued that rather than pleasure, acceptance or superiority, the main drive of an individual was in finding meaning in life.

118) White noise machines are useful to

   A) Downplay any distracting background noise outside an office
   B) Create a light and playful environment
   C) Increase the client's sense of privacy and comfort
   D) Both A and C

The correct answer is D:) Both A and C. Although it is important to be aware of specific patient needs as some patients will be annoyed by these, many will feel more comfortable in the "quieter" environment and feel like their privacy is more protected.

119) If the primary concern of a researcher were that their observations are an accurate reflection of how individual's react in normal situations, which type of observation would they wish to employ?

   A) Subjective observation
   B) Structured observation
   C) Unobtrusive observation
   D) Astute observation

The correct answer is C:) Unobtrusive observation. Unobtrusive observation is also referred to as naturalistic observation.

120) The first IQ test was the

   A) Simon-Binet scale
   B) RIASEC
   C) Rorschach Inkblot Test
   D) DSM-IV

The correct answer is A:) Simon-Binet scale. The test was meant to be used in schools to determine which children should be placed in special classrooms for mental retardation.

121) A counselor who treats their close friend constitutes an unethical dual relationship if

   A) They have known the friend for more than seven years
   B) The friend is of the opposite gender
   C) The relationship has the potential to impair objectivity or effectiveness, and could be harmful to their friend
   D) All of the above

The correct answer is C:) The relationship has the potential to impair objectivity or effectiveness, and could be harmful to their friend. Although dual relationships are not always illegal or unethical, they should be avoided if at all possible.

122) Carol Gilligan worked as a research assistant under

   A) Karl Abraham
   B) Lawrence Kohlberg
   C) Sigmund Freud
   D) Abraham Maslow

The correct answer is B:) Lawrence Kohlberg. Lawrence Kohlberg is known for his theory of moral development. Gilligan herself focused on the moral development of women.

123) Which of the following would be the most advisable in a counselor's office?

   A) Absolute minimal ornamentation
   B) Pillows and rugs
   C) Monochromatic, box-like furniture
   D) Smooth, sleek surfaces

The correct answer is B:) Pillows and rugs. These elements tend to create a softer feel, which ads to client comfort. Displaying credentials and other important information is also advisable.

124) Most states require a minimum of a _____ degree in order for a person to become a counselor.

   A) Masters
   B) Bachelors
   C) Doctorate
   D) High School Diploma

The correct answer is A:) Masters. In addition, many states also require a certain number of clinical hours and different forms of licensure in order for a person to practice as a counselor.

125) Which of the following is NOT affected by the specific type of counseling that a person does?

   A) Average pay
   B) Working environment
   C) Education requirements
   D) All of the above are affected on what type of counselor one becomes

The correct answer is D:) All of the above are affected by what type of counselor one becomes. The field of counseling involves a wide range of activities, pays, licensure requirements, and working environments.

126) Which of the following treatments are associated with holistic therapy?

   A) Yoga
   B) Acupuncture
   C) Nutrition
   D) All of the above

The correct answer is D:) All of the above. Holistic therapy takes a variety of approaches involving mind, body, and spirit in the healing process.

127) According to Jung's analytical perspective

A) People are influenced solely by their unconscious sexual drives.
B) People are influenced by feelings of inferiority in three major areas of life.
C) People are influenced primarily by a human desire to progress.
D) People are influenced primarily by mid-life events and the influence of person and collective unconscious thoughts.

The correct answer is D:) People are influenced primarily by mid-life events and the influence of personal and collective unconscious thoughts. Jung's theories differ from Freud's (who focused on young life and sexual urges) in these regards.

128) Which of the following therapies would NOT be considered humanistic?

A) Client-centered therapy
B) Structuralist therapy
C) Logotherapy
D) Gestalt therapy

The correct answer is B:) Structuralist therapy. The goal of structuralism is to break down the functions of the mind into their most basic components, requiring a very different perspective than the humanistic view of considering all situations individually.

129) A client is struggling with their self-esteem, and feels as though it is causing them to stagnate in their work sphere. What would a counselor suggest if considering the situation from a humanistic perspective?

A) Finding ways to improve their self-esteem because it has become a barrier to their natural desire for progression and freedom.
B) Spending a day at the spa because it is likely a physical problem more than it is an emotional or psychological one.
C) Taking some sort of medication because it is most likely that there is a medical reason that they feel restricted and unable to progress.
D) Recognizing that low self-esteem is a fact of life that they need to learn how to work around to become more satisfied with their work.

The correct answer is A:) Finding ways to improve their self-esteem because it has become a barrier to their natural desire for progression and freedom. Humanistic theory advocates the concept that human beings have an innate desire for growth. Therapists help to remove these barriers.

130) The ACA is the

   A) Accepted Counseling Academy
   B) American Counseling Association
   C) Allowable Counseling Practice Board
   D) None of the above

The correct answer is B:) American Counseling Association.

131) According to Gilligan, women place stronger emphasis on _____ in moral decision making.

   A) Relationships
   B) Caring
   C) Individual rights and responsibility
   D) Both A & B

The correct answer is D:) Both A & B. Gilligan's research showed that women place stronger emphasis on relationships and caring in moral decision making.

132) Which division of the APA represents counseling psychology?

   A) Division 17
   B) Division 34
   C) Division 1
   D) Division 15

The correct answer is A:) Division 17. The APA is represented by 54 different which represent specific categories or interests of psychology divisions.

133) The intimacy vs. isolation conflict occurs during

   A) Play age
   B) Adolescence
   C) Early adulthood
   D) Adulthood

The correct answer is C:) Early adulthood. Beginning at age 20, young adults experience relationships and search for love.

134) Which of the following is NOT a concern relative to co-leaders in group therapy?

   A) Power struggles
   B) Incompatible styles
   C) Decrease in effectiveness of therapy
   D) All of the above are concerns

The correct answer is C:) Decrease in effectiveness of therapy. Group therapy is often more effective with two leaders because it allows more interaction between members and leaders.

135) Which of the following is TRUE about the advocacy role of a counselor?

   A) Counselors should develop communication, organization, and collaborative skills to be most competent advocates for their clients.
   B) Counselors should focus on having a sympathetic and willing disposition in order to be an effective advocate for their clients.
   C) Counselors should have a wide knowledge base which includes an understanding of advocacy techniques and the resources available to their clients.
   D) All of the above

The correct answer is D:) All of the above. In order to be most effective as an advocate for clients, it is important that counselors develop the necessary disposition, knowledge, and skills to do so.

136) A counselor working to connect a client with resources available to them that are directly related to their needs is advocating at which level?

   A) Community/systems
   B) World
   C) Individual
   D) Public/societal

The correct answer is C:) Individual. This most fundamental level of advocacy involves examining the situations directly creating barriers for the client, and working to remove those barriers. One of the most common barriers faced by individuals is a lack of access to needed resources.

137) When a client takes emotions that they may have associated with another significant individual or situation and unconsciously shifts them to the therapist it is referred to as

A) DSM-IV
B) Rational-emotive behavioral shift
C) Transference
D) Countertransference

The correct answer is C:) Transference. When the opposite occurs (i.e., the counselor's feelings are shifted onto the client) it is referred to as countertransference.

138) Transference was first studied by

A) Freud
B) Piaget
C) Rogers
D) Skinner

The correct answer is A:) Freud. He was led to study it when a female client threw her arms around him.

139) Which of the following is NOT a proper use of silence in therapy?

A) To give patients a chance both to consider their feelings and to better verbalize them.
B) To convey a sense of empathy, understanding, and respect for the patient.
C) To encourage quiet patients to verbalize their emotions.
D) All of the above describe proper uses of silence in therapy.

The correct answer is D:) All of the above describe proper uses of silence in therapy. However, a counselor should be aware that in some situations silence is more detrimental than helpful.

140) Section 504 of the Rehabilitation Act is most often applied to

A) Transportation issues for disabled individuals
B) Sexual harassment of clients by therapists
C) Building accessibility issues for disabled individuals
D) Payment of rehabilitation centers by elderly individuals needing care

The correct answer is A:) Transportation issues for disabled individuals. The act specifically applies to transportation to and from activities or programs funded by the federal government.

141) Which of the following requires that all federally funded buildings are accessible to disabled individuals?

   A) Section 504 of the Rehabilitation Act
   B) Americans with Disabilities Act
   C) Section 502 of the Rehabilitation Act
   D) Accessible Design Act

The correct answer is C:) Section 502 of the Rehabilitation Act. The Americans with Disabilities Act extends this requirement to any public buildings.

142) Which of the following is an important characteristic for a counselor to exhibit?

   A) Open; personable and accepting of client shortcomings
   B) Selfless; focus on needs and concerns of counselors
   C) Reliable; a healthy balance between consistency and flexibility
   D) All of the above

The correct answer is D:) All of the above. Additional characteristics that counselors should exhibit are self-confidence, self-awareness, good leadership, empathy, and genuineness. Counselors should avoid excessive storytelling, and preaching.

143) A therapist would be most likely to use the silent treatment with

   A) Patients suffering from abuse issues
   B) Proactive, problem-oriented clients
   C) Emotionally disturbed patients
   D) Unresponsive patients

The correct answer is B:) Proactive, problem oriented clients. Silence is typically considered to be safest and most effective for these clients, whereas it is not used with clients who have severe or deep set emotional issues or disturbances.

144) Alcoholics Anonymous began in the

   A) 1920s
   B) 1930s
   C) 1940s
   D) 1950s

The correct answer is B:) 1930s. AA began with two men who recovered from their alcoholism and began to help other alcoholics.

145) Which of the following is TRUE regarding drink and drug consumption among minors?

    A) Teens are consuming drugs and alcohol at progressively younger ages.
    B) Teen drug consumption has not changed with time.
    C) Teens are consuming drugs and alcohol at progressively older ages.
    D) Fewer teens are experimenting with drugs as time progresses.

The correct answer is A:) Teens are consuming drugs and alcohol at progressively younger ages. This is one of the most worrisome factors of drug consumption.

146) Which of the following is NOT a technique used in feminist therapy?

    A) Gender-role analysis
    B) Power analysis and intervention
    C) Differentiation
    D) Reframing and relabeling

The correct answer is C:) Differentiation. Differentiation relates to the independence of individuals in a family situation.

147) Which of the following statements is FALSE?

    A) Religion has little influence in the lives of most individuals.
    B) Counselors do not need to be aware of issues regarding a patient's spiritual beliefs.
    C) A client's spiritual beliefs are always a useful tool in the recovery process.
    D) All of the above

The correct answer is D:) All of the above. The vast majority of people in the United States identify themselves with some form of religion. Sometimes religion can be a useful tool in the recovery process, and other times it may be harmful. In any case it is important that a counselor be aware of issues regarding a patient's spiritual beliefs.

148) Which of the following studied operant conditioning?

    A) Alfred Kinsey
    B) Carl Jung
    C) B. F. Skinner
    D) Carl Rogers

The correct answer is C:) B. F. Skinner.

149) Which of the following is an example of Maslow's first level of needs?

   A) Food
   B) School
   C) Car
   D) Travel

The correct answer is A:) Food.

150) Assessment is to process as testing is to

   A) Product
   B) Result
   C) Specific event
   D) Long procedure

The correct answer is C:) Specific event. Whereas assessment is a process which incorporates many aspects of counseling, testing is essentially a snapshot in time to gather concise information.

151) Which of the following is NOT an aspect of the cognitive domain?

   A) Fact recollection
   B) General intelligence
   C) Personality
   D) Aptitude

The correct answer is C:) Personality. Personality is an aspect of the affective domain (which involves non-cognitive measures).

152) Which axis of the DSM-IV do personality disorders belong to?

   A) Axis I
   B) Axis II
   C) Axis III
   D) Axis IV

The correct answer is B:) Axis II. Axis II of the DSM-IV includes personality and developmental disorders.

153) An individual scores a 20% on a test one day and an 80% on the same type of test the next day. This test has a problem with

　　A) Test reliability
　　B) Test understandability
　　C) Test validity
　　D) None of the above

The correct answer is A:) Test reliability. If the test cannot give a consistent score for the same individual, then it is unreliable.

154) Which of the following is NOT one of the forms of dysfunctional communication identified by Virginia Satir?

　　A) Distractor
　　B) Blamer
　　C) Asserter
　　D) Placator

The correct answer is C:) Asserter. The four types of dysfunctional communicators within a family are the distractor, the computer, the placator, and the blamer.

155) Which of the following is NOT one of the steps in the 12 step program?

　　A) Making amends
　　B) Achieving sobriety
　　C) Taking moral inventory
　　D) Prayer and meditation

The correct answer is B:) Achieving sobriety. A, C, and D are steps 9, 4, and 11 of the 12 step program.

156) Which of the following is NOT a primary goal of the APA?

　　A) Ensure and increase organizational effectiveness
　　B) Advocate the role of school counselors in educational settings
　　C) Expand and validate psychology as a profession
　　D) Establish psychology as a scientific endeavor

The correct answer is B:) Advocate the role of school counselors in educational settings. The three stated primary goals of the APA are described by answers A, C, and D.

157) Which of the following individuals incorporated emotional fusion as a part of their theories?

A) Satir
B) Freud
C) Erikson
D) Bowen

The correct answer is D:) Bowen. According to Bowen, in a state of emotional fusion no distinction or balance between emotions and feelings. This leads to a tenuous situation within family units.

158) Triangulation (or triangular relationships) is an important element of which type of counseling?

A) Family counseling
B) Mental health counseling
C) Substance abuse counseling
D) Advocacy counseling

The correct answer is A:) Family counseling. Both Satir and Bowen studied the effects of triangular relationships between parents and children on the functioning of the family as a whole.

159) Which type of therapy would most likely be preferred by a drug user?

A) Structuralist therapy
B) Vocational therapy
C) Group therapy
D) Person-centered

The correct answer is C:) Group therapy. Group therapy allows a sense of community and support to develop.

160) Which theory classifies personalities based on generally understood characteristics?

A) Gestalt theory
B) Functionalism
C) Structuralism
D) Trait and factor theory

The correct answer is D:) Trait and factor theory. These characteristics are referred to as traits.

161) Which of the following could be considered an advocate?

A) Parent
B) Counselor
C) Close friend
D) All of the above

The correct answer is D:) All of the above. Advocates are people who care about an individual, and who help them through their counseling process. Counselors can and should become powerful advocates for their clients when necessary and possible.

162) If a counselor becomes aware of a colleague acting unethically, their first step should be to

A) Inform their client
B) Inform the ACA
C) Try to resolve the issue with them directly
D) Expose their conduct to media sources

The correct answer is C:) Try to resolve the issue with them directly. If there is concern that the unethical actions may result in harm for a client it should then be reported to the appropriate state and national committees, licensing boards and other concerned parties.

163) Which of the following is a decision approach to career development?

A) Trait and factor theory
B) Expectancy theory
C) Maslow's theory of self-actualization
D) Roe's developmental model

The correct answer is B:) Expectancy theory. The two important decision approaches are expectancy theory and self-efficacy theory.

164) The paradoxical intention technique of logotherapy is best described as

A) Active, questioning dialogue meant to help clients gain perspective.
B) An attempt to overemphasize a problem or phobia to eliminate a client's fear of it.
C) A distraction technique which attempts to draw attention away from the problem.
D) A phenomenon in which clients irrationally fear the counseling process.

The correct answer is B:) An attempt to overemphasize a problem or phobia to eliminate a client's fear of it. Socratic dialogue (answer A) and dereflection (answer C) are also techniques used in logotherapy.

165) The term in phenomenology which describes a person's unique perceptions of the world is

A) Qualia
B) Imperative
C) Individualism
D) Quatrain

The correct answer is A:) Qualia. For example, a phenomenological individual may question whether each person experiences the color red in the same way, or if they taste food the same.

166) Which of the following is NOT one of the three basic musts identified by Ellis in REBT?

A) The approval of others determines self-worth
B) Those who treat you unfairly are inherently bad
C) Success is measured by individual happiness
D) Life should be easy

The correct answer is C:) Success is measured by individual happiness. Answers A, B, and D constitute the three basic musts which Ellis identified as detrimental thought processes.

167) Which of the following therapy types would be most likely to incorporate psychotherapy, good nutrition, and Pilates?

   A) Psychodynamic therapy
   B) Multicultural therapy
   C) Holistic therapy
   D) Gestalt therapy

The correct answer is C:) Holistic therapy. Holistic therapy incorporates a variety of techniques which consider physical, mental and spiritual health along with traditional therapy methods.

168) Which of the following is TRUE regarding multicultural therapy?

   A) Counselors should approach their clients with no values or culture of their own, just to be safe.
   B) A counselor should not treat patients based on stereotypes because all individuals are different.
   C) It is advisable for counselors to push their own views onto patients to help them feel more included.
   D) None of the above

The correct answer is B:) A counselor should not treat patients based on stereotypes because all individuals are different. Although it is important for counselors to be aware of cultural norms and expectations, they should also not be locked into stereotypic views.

169) A client is struggling with their self-esteem, and feels as though it is causing them to stagnate in their work sphere. What would a counselor suggest if considering the situation from a humanistic perspective?

   A) Find ways to improve their self-esteem because it has become a barrier to their natural desire for progression and freedom.
   B) Spending a day at the spa because it is likely a physical problem more than it is an emotional or psychological one.
   C) Take some sort of medication because it is most likely that there is a medical reason that they feel restricted and unable to progress.
   D) Recognizing that low self-esteem is a fact of their life and that they need to learn how to work around it to become more satisfied with their work.

The correct answer is D:) Recognizing that low self-esteem is a fact of their life and that they need to learn how to work around it to become more satisfied with their work. Existential therapy encourages individuals to recognize the limitations and restrictions in their lives, and to find ways for growth and fulfillment in spite of them.

170) A counselor attempts to truly understand their patient's feelings, perspectives and situations, rather than simply feeling sorry for them. They are showing

   A) Sympathy
   B) Apathy
   C) Eclecticism
   D) Empathy

The correct answer is D:) Empathy. Sympathy would involve a feeling of pity rather than understanding.

171) Which of the following would be the most preferred trait for a counselor to possess?

   A) Empathy
   B) Sympathy
   C) Pity
   D) Stoicism

The correct answer is A:) Empathy. Empathy describes when one person sees that another is suffering and tries to better understand them. This makes it a critical skill for a counselor to have.

172) A girl is abused by her father and later in life transfers negative characteristics to anyone who looks like him. This is an example of

   A) Parataxic distortion
   B) Tarasoff approach
   C) Post-judgmentalism
   D) Symptomatology

The correct answer is A:) Parataxic distortion. This is when one person views another person in a skewed way based on either their own fictional concept of how the person should be, or their association with another person.

173) Which was the first state to require professional licensure for counselors?

   A) Massachusetts
   B) New York
   C) California
   D) Connecticut

The correct answer is D:) Connecticut. Requirements began in 1945 with the state of Connecticut. Shortly following these licensure requirements in Connecticut, the state of California began to require the registration of counselors and psychologists, and other states followed.

174) An advocate would generally NOT

   A) Encourage a person to seek counseling
   B) Attend counseling sessions with an individual to help them
   C) Criticize and insult an individual
   D) Be supportive and understanding of an individual's struggles

The correct answer is C:) Criticize and insult an individual. Advocates are people who care about an individual, and who help them through their counseling process.

175) The most widely used code of ethics is published by the

   A) U.S. Government
   B) American Psychiatric Association
   C) American Counseling Association
   D) Ethical Counseling Board

The correct answer is C:) American Counseling Association.

176) Which of the following is most influential in how meaning is interpreted?

   A) Verbal communication factors
   B) Nonverbal communication factors
   C) Eye contact
   D) None of the above

The correct answer is B:) Nonverbal communication factors. Actions speak louder than words, and when there is a different in verbal and nonverbal signals, a person will typically react to the nonverbal signals.

177) Which of the following does NOT characterize Adlerian counseling?

A) An open and trusting relationship between counselor and client.
B) A goal of changing the client's belief system to a more correct and healthy one.
C) An emphasis on behavior modification to eliminate client feelings of superiority.
D) Neither A nor C is a characteristic of Adlerian counseling.

The correct answer is C:) An emphasis on behavior modification to eliminate client feelings of superiority. Adlerian philosophy works to elevate patients from feelings of inferiority, not the other way around.

178) In order to be effective, it is most important that a counselor

A) Employ the best strategy for a particular situation.
B) Build a strong and genuine relationship with the patient.
C) Has a lifestyle similar to that of the client.
D) Has a strong understanding of their own inadequacies.

The correct answer is B:) Build a strong and genuine relationship with the patient.

179) Which of the following is NOT a commonly used consultation model?

A) Mental health
B) Structural
C) Training workshop
D) Behavioral

The correct answer is B:) Structural. The most common consultation models are mental health, training workshop, behavioral, and process.

180) Donald Super is known for his theories regarding

A) Mental illness
B) Career development
C) Racial prejudice
D) Counselor confidentiality laws

The correct answer is B:) Career development. Donald Super is known for his theories in career development. He described five stages that individuals progress through during their lives, and the aspects of each career phase.

181) A group which includes all teenage girls suffering from eating disorders would best be described as

   A) Heterogeneous
   B) Homogenous
   C) Eclectic
   D) Static

The correct answer is B:) Homogenous.

182) A counselor is hired by an organization to analyze and improve the communication structure of the organization. The consultation model best described by the situation is the

   A) Mental health model
   B) Training workshop model
   C) Behavioral model
   D) Process model

The correct answer is D:) Process model. The process model is mainly focused with organizational structures. The consultant in this model is essentially an expert in organizational development.

183) Shaping occurs in stages referred to as

   A) Successive approximations
   B) Qualia
   C) Differentiators
   D) Capacities

The correct answer is A:) Successive approximations. Shaping involves reinforcing gradual changes towards a desired behavior. Each stage is a successive approximation in the process.

184) Congruence is an important element in which type of theories?

   A) Humanistic
   B) Psychoanalytic
   C) Behavioral
   D) None of the above

The correct answer is A:) Humanistic. In humanistic theories the most important trait for a counselor to possess is referred to as congruence.

185) Which of the following terms is NOT interchangeable with the others?

   A) Genuineness
   B) Eclecticism
   C) Authenticity
   D) Congruence

The correct answer is B:) Eclecticism. Genuineness, authenticity and congruence all refer to counselors appearing as real and caring individuals to their clients.

186) Edmund Husserl is associated with which approach to therapy?

   A) Structuralist
   B) Phenomenological
   C) Gestalt
   D) Holistic

The correct answer is B:) Phenomenological.

187) The work of Frederick and Laura Perls is associated with

   A) Gestalt therapy
   B) Holistic therapy
   C) Psychodynamic therapy
   D) Rational emotive behavioral therapy

The correct answer is A:) Gestalt therapy.

188) Which individual is most associated with person-centered therapy?

   A) Carl Rogers
   B) Jean Piaget
   C) P.F. Skinner
   D) Viktor Frankel

The correct answer is A:) Carl Rogers.

189) Which of the following is NOT an importance premise of logotherapy?

   A) All life has meaning
   B) People have a will to meaning
   C) People must be taught a will to meaning
   D) People can active their will to meaning and pursue a better life

The correct answer is C:) People must be taught a will to meaning. Answers A, B and D are the three main premises of logotherapy.

190) Members of Alcoholics Anonymous

   A) Attend meetings
   B) Implement the 12 step program
   C) Share their experiences
   D) All of the above

The correct answer is D:) All of the above. Men and women in the AA program implement a "twelve step program" to treat their addiction and attend meetings to share their experiences with alcohol.

191) Which of the following would NOT be considered an instinct in instinct theory?

   A) Hunger
   B) Reproduction
   C) Writing
   D) Blinking

The correct answer is C:) Writing. Writing is a learned behavior, therefore not an instinct.

192) A wife is upset with her husband and rather than discuss the problem with him, she complains to a friend. This is an example of

   A) Symptomatology
   B) Transference
   C) Triangulation
   D) Ethnocentrism

The correct answer is C:) Triangulation. Triangulation occurs when an individual vents to an unrelated third party about a conflict with another person. Although it offers temporary relief, in the long run triangulation is typically destructive.

193) Which of the following is characteristic of the consulting relationship?

   A) Hierarchical
   B) Mandatory
   C) Collaborative
   D) All of the above

The correct answer is C:) Collaborative. Consulting is a non-hierarchical, voluntary, and collaborative approach to problem solving when a counselor encounters a difficult case.

194) A person who views their own culture as superior to all others is said to be

   A) Acculturated
   B) Egocentric
   C) Stereotypical
   D) Ethnocentric

The correct answer is D:) Ethnocentric. A person with an ethnocentric mindset will often view their own culture as dominant and then rank all others in relation to it. Ethnocentricity will often lead to stereotyping and racism.

195) Which of the following identifies Donald Super's five stages of career development in their correct order?

   A) Growth, fantasy, maintenance, exploration, and decline
   B) Exploration, growth, maintenance, generativity, and decline
   C) Growth, exploration, establishment, maintenance, and decline
   D) Exploration, establishment, conservation, decline, and fantasy

The correct answer is C:) Growth, exploration, establishment, maintenance, and decline. According to Super, individuals progress in order through each phase during the course of their lives.

196) The study of symptoms that can be used to diagnose diseases is

   A) Deinstitutionalization
   B) Logotherapy
   C) Medicatrics
   D) Symptomatology

The correct answer is D:) Symptomatology. Symptomatology takes an important role in counseling because often psychological problems will begin to manifest themselves physically and can be identified in no other way.

197) The Tarasoff case established the counselors

   A) Duty to treat
   B) Duty to counsel
   C) Duty to warn
   D) Duty to detain

The correct answer is C:) Duty to warn. In this case, the court ruled that because of a therapist's special relationship with their patients, they do have a duty to warn individuals who are in danger of imminent harm from patients.

198) Polysubstance abuse is defined as the

   A) Abuse of two different drugs over a number of years
   B) Abuse of three or more drugs indiscriminately for a year
   C) Abuse of multiple substances at any single point
   D) Abuse of three or more drugs for two months

The correct answer is B:) Abuse of three or more drugs indiscriminately for a year. Polysubstance abuse is a condition in which an individual is addicted to or abusing three or more drugs on a regular basis over a period of 12 months. The drugs are used indiscriminately, meaning that no single drug is considered the favorite or primary drug used.

199) A therapist uses multiple theories when treating a patient. This would be described as

   A) Gestalt therapy
   B) Eclecticism
   C) Logotherapy
   D) Symptomatology

The correct answer is B:) Eclecticism. Eclecticism is characterized by combining a number of different approaches in treatment.

200) Which of the following does NOT describe counselor congruence?

   A) Genuine
   B) Authentic
   C) Sincere
   D) Symptomatic

The correct answer is D:) Symptomatic. Genuineness, authenticity and congruence all refer to counselors appearing as real and caring individuals to their clients.

201) In which of the following situations would a counselor NOT be ethically justified in breaking confidentiality?

   A) When the client is determined to be a danger to themselves
   B) If the client has seriously threatened the counselor's life
   C) When the client confesses plans to kill another person
   D) If the client is cheating on their spouse

The correct answer is D:) If the client is cheating on their spouse. Counselors owe a duty of care and protection to those who are in situations of immediate threat of violence by patients. In most situations, however, they owe a duty of confidentiality to their patients.

202) The most important organization involved with accrediting counseling programs is the

   A) NBCC
   B) APA
   C) CACREP
   D) ACA

The correct answer is C:) CACREP. The CACREP is the Council for Accreditation of Counseling and Related Education Programs.

203) Systems therapy

   A) Considers the interconnectedness of individuals in a population
   B) Was originally applied to the field of chemistry
   C) Advocates an individualistic perspective
   D) All of the above

The correct answer is A:) Considers the interconnectedness of individuals in a population. It was first advocated by a biologist in studying cells, and advocates a community-minded perspective.

204) Which of the following is NOT characteristic of active listening?

   A) Nodding
   B) Texting
   C) Open posture
   D) Eye contact

The correct answer is B:) Texting. This would be destructive to the conversation rather than aiding in effective and active listening.

205) Paraphrasing is one technique of

   A) Active listening
   B) Cursory listening
   C) Public speaking
   D) Effective citation

The correct answer is A:) Active listening. Active listening involves making a concerted effort to understand what a person is saying. Paraphrasing can be a powerful technique in which one person repeats back what was said in their own words. It allows for clarification and increased understanding.

206) A therapist seeks to show a patient that they truly care about his or her life. This is an example of

   A) Genuineness
   B) Paraphrasing
   C) Deinstitutionalization
   D) Active listening

The correct answer is A:) Genuineness. Genuineness, authenticity and congruence all refer to counselors appearing as real and caring individuals to their clients. Counseling is most effective when patients feel that the counselor genuinely cares about them.

207) Which of the following best describes the deinstitutionalization movement?

   A) A movement towards placing patients in long-term, stated-owned facilities
   B) A movement towards putting patients through short-term holistic counseling
   C) A movement towards placing patients in localized community facilities offering outpatient care
   D) A movement towards ignoring mental illnesses and denying treatment to those suffering from them

The correct answer is C:) A movement towards placing patients in localized community facilities offering outpatient care. This was a result of the under-funding of state programs, inadequacy of care, and the development of psychiatric medicine which made perpetual treatment unnecessary for some patients.

208) If a person has the opinion that "all foreign food is gross," they could be described as having which perspective?

   A) Ethnocentric
   B) Cultural relativist
   C) Egotistical
   D) Racist

The correct answer is A:) Ethnocentric. Ethnocentrism is a perspective of viewing the world through the lens of an individual's own ethnicity or culture. In ethnocentrism, an individual believes that their own culture and beliefs are superior to all others. Believing that "all foreign food is gross" is one example of placing one's own cultural norms above that of others.

209) Which of the following is NOT one of the three main branches through which counseling developed as a profession?

   A) Clinical psychology
   B) Vocational counseling
   C) Psychotherapy
   D) Counseling psychology

The correct answer is C:) Psychotherapy. Although psychotherapy was one of the important first elements of counseling psychology, answers A, B, and D are the three main branches.

210) Ginzberg's career development theory involves three phases: fantasy, tentative, and realistic. Which phase is marked by a sense of urgency about making career choices?

   A) Fantasy
   B) Tentative
   C) Realistic
   D) Both A and B

The correct answer is B:) Tentative. During this phase, individuals begin to have a greater understanding of various jobs and requirements, and begin to realize the potential for fulfillment that they offer.

211) What is the new name for American Association for Counseling?

    A) Association for Counseling in America
    B) America's Counseling Association
    C) American Counseling Association
    D) Counseling Association of America

The correct answer is C:) American Counseling Association. The American Counseling Association (ACA) is a professional and educational organization.

212) Instinct theory is a theory of

    A) Moral development
    B) Motivation
    C) Behavior
    D) Biological impulses

The correct answer is B:) Motivation. Instinct theory is a theory of motivation which attempts to explain human behavior.

213) The A-B-C model is associated with which theory?

    A) Holistic therapy
    B) Rational emotive behavior therapy
    C) Gestalt therapy
    D) Cognitive therapy

The correct answer is B:) Rational emotive behavior theory. REBT operates under the assumption that beliefs ("B") cause emotions, not situations ("A").

214) Career Development Theories fall into the four categories of trait factor, _____, decision, and developmental.

    A) Sociology
    B) Psychological
    C) Personality
    D) Developmental psychology

The correct answer is B:) Psychological. This particular category was introduced by John Lewis Holland in the 1980s. Holland was an American psychologist and professor who created the career development model known as the Holland Codes from which the psychological category is derived.

215) Of Dr. Camara Jones' three levels of racism, _____ is categorized as the differences in access to goods, services, and opportunities afforded to a particular race in society.

A) Institutional racism
B) Personally mediated racism
C) Internalized racism
D) Interminority racism

The correct answer is A:) Institutional racism. Personally mediated racism refers to the thought process that abilities, motives, and intentions are different according to race, which results in differential treatment to members of that particular race. Internalized racism refers to the acceptance of an ostracized race of the negative messages about their own capabilities and overall worth. Interminority racism refers to the discrimination found between racial minorities.

216) _____ is one of the six conditions, identified by psychologist Carl Rogers, needed to produce personality change in clients as part of his person-centered therapy approach.

A) Counselor or therapist conditional positive regard
B) Counselor or therapist sympathetic understanding
C) Client misconception
D) Counselor or therapist congruence

The correct answer is D:) Counselor or therapist congruence. This condition refers to the therapist becoming deeply involved in the therapy, meaning they draw from their own personal experiences in order to create a stronger relationship with the client.

217) Both Gestalt therapy and narrative theory deal with the patient as whole, but where Gestalt therapy seeks to solve an issue through assimilation, narrative therapy uses _____ to provide solutions.

A) The dialogue game
B) Introjection
C) Deconstruction
D) Organismic self-regulation

The correct answer is C:) Deconstruction. The other three answers refer to Gestalt therapy.

218) _____ is the act of administering the same test twice to a group of people in order to evaluate the stability of the test.

   A) Test-retest stability
   B) Test-retest reliability
   C) Test-retest validity
   D) Test-retest maintainability

The correct answer is B:) Test-retest reliability. The other three answers are just variations on the right answer.

219) _____ is the best reference material for career development.

   A) Encyclopedia Britannica
   B) Encyclopedia of Counseling
   C) Encyclopedia of Social Work
   D) Encyclopedia of Career Development

The correct answer is D:) Encyclopedia of Career Development. Introduced by SAGE Reference, the Encyclopedia of Career Development has over 400 articles all relating to career topics.

220) _____ was a social worker known as the founder of career or vocational counseling.

   A) Frank Parsons
   B) Jane Addams
   C) Fritz Perls
   D) Michael White

The correct answer is A:) Frank Parsons. Frank Parsons was influenced by Jane Addams. Fritz Perls was one of the creators of Gestalt therapy and Michael White was one of the creators of narrative therapy.

221) Integrative psychotherapy refers to the therapeutic process of integrating a patient's personality or uniting specific personality traits within a patient. The second route of integration is commonly referred to as _____, or the improvement of our ability to select the appropriate treatment for a patient in relation to a specific problem.

A) Common factors
B) Theoretical integration
C) Technical eclecticism
D) Assimilative integration

The correct answer is C:) Technical eclecticism. The other three options are the first, third, and fourth routes of integration.

222) During a child's development, there are generally three major timeframes that are identified as periods where a child develops and acquires an understanding of values. Those periods are the _____ period, the modeling period, and the socialization period.

A) Pre-moral
B) Principled
C) Conventional
D) Imprinting

The correct answer is D:) Imprinting. The imprinting period occurs from birth up to the age of seven and is the time when children absorb everything around them.

223) _____ is a form of abuse that subjects an individual to psychological trauma and not physical trauma.

A) Emotional/verbal abuse
B) Intrapersonal abuse
C) Codependent abuse
D) Interpersonal abuse

The correct answer is A:) Emotional/verbal abuse. This form of abuse is usually conducted without physically harming a person. Instead, it employs methods such as bullying that can lead to post-traumatic stress disorder, depression, or anxiety.

224) A counselor may choose to avoid eye contact with a client because _____.

   A) It can show a client you are really interested in what they have to say.
   B) It may be considered disrespectful or hostile in certain cultures.
   C) They find blinking distracts their patients.
   D) They find it makes them laugh.

The correct answer is B:) It may be considered disrespectful or hostile in certain cultures. There are many reasons why a counselor may choose to avoid eye contact based upon their client interaction, but one of the main reasons can be related to cultural beliefs. Some cultures find making direct eye contact disrespectful, hostile, or even flirtatious.

225) Psychodynamic therapy focuses on revealing the _____ content of a client's mind in order to alleviate tension.

   A) Unconscious
   B) Conscious
   C) Biometric
   D) None of the above

The correct answer is A:) Unconscious. The overall goal of psychodynamic therapy is to identify certain unconscious acts in a person's current behavior in order to make them aware of how the past can influence their current behavior.

226) Patient confidentiality is key to building and maintaining trust between a counselor and a patient; however, it can be breached under specific circumstances, including patient consent, _____, and in the interest of the public.

   A) When the law requires it
   B) When a therapist decides it is time
   C) When a priest decides it is time
   D) None of the above

The correct answer is A:) When the law requires it. There are certain instances when confidentiality can be breached in accordance with the law.

227) _____ has three core conditions that must be met to produce a personality change in patients. They are congruence, unconditional positive regard, and empathy.

   A) Narrative therapy
   B) Gestalt therapy
   C) Cognitive therapy
   D) Person-centered therapy

The correct answer is D:) Person-centered therapy. Created by Carl Rogers, person-centered therapy focuses on a client's ability to self-actualize.

228) Based on theories from Alfred Adler, Adlerian therapy is managed in four stages, with the first stage working to create a _____ relationship between a patient and therapist.

   A) Symbiotic
   B) Distant
   C) Collaborative
   D) Motivated

The correct answer is C:) Collaborative. Alderian therapy focuses on the development of an individual's personality and understanding how it connects to all individuals. This type of therapy is not successful unless there is a strong connection between patient and counselor.

229) According to the National Institute on Drug Abuse, alcohol, tobacco, and _____ are the most abused drugs by adolescents.

   A) Ecstasy
   B) Vicodin
   C) Cocaine
   D) Marijuana

The correct answer is D:) Marijuana. The other three options are also abused by adolescents, but are not among the most abused.

230) Conceived by Dr. Murray Bowen, _____ is a therapeutic approach that views family as key to an individual's problems and seeks to resolve those issues by having family members work together to understand their role in the family dynamic.

    A) Family systems therapy
    B) Narrative therapy
    C) Gestalt therapy
    D) None of the above

The correct answer is A:) Family systems therapy. The other two options focus more on the individual as a whole rather than the family aspect.

231) _____ is a therapeutic approach that observes a client's responses to a set of specifically constructed questions and uses those responses to refocus a client's mindset.

    A) Family system therapy
    B) Cognitive therapy
    C) Narrative therapy
    D) Solution-focused theory

The correct answer is D:) Solution-focused theory. This approach is specifically focused on getting the patient to explore their history and current issues by using a set of questions geared to guiding a patient through these areas of their life.

 ## Test-Taking Strategies

Here are some test-taking strategies that are specific to this test and to other DSST tests in general:

- Keep your eyes on the time. Pay attention to how much time you have left.
- Read the entire question and read all the answers. Many questions are not as hard to answer as they may seem. Sometimes, a difficult sounding question really only is asking you how to read an accompanying chart. Chart and graph questions are on most DANTES/DSST tests and should be an easy free point.
- If you don't know the answer immediately, the new computer-based testing lets you mark questions and come back to them later if you have time.
- Read the wording carefully. Some words can give you hints to the right answer. There are no exceptions to an answer when there are words in the question such as always, all or none. If one of the answer choices includes most or some of the right answers, but not all, then that is not the answer. Here is an example:

    The primary colors include all of the following:

    A) Red, Yellow, Blue, Green

    B) Red, Green, Yellow

    C) Red, Orange, Yellow

    D) Red, Yellow, Blue

    Although item A includes all the right answers, it also includes an incorrect answer, making it incorrect. If you didn't read it carefully, was in a hurry, or didn't know the material well, you might fall for this.

- Make a guess on a question that you do not know the answer to. There is no penalty for an incorrect answer. Eliminate the answer choices that you know are incorrect. For example, this will let your guess be a 1 in 3 chance instead.

 ## Test Preparation

How much you need to study depends on your knowledge of a subject area. If you are interested in literature, took it in school, or enjoy reading then your study and preparation for the literature or humanities test will not need to be as intensive as that of someone who is new to literature.

This book is much different than the regular DANTES study guides. This book actually teaches you the information that you need to know to pass the test. If you are particularly interested in an area, or feel that you want more information, do a quick search online. We've tried not to include too much depth in areas that are not as essential on the test. Everything in this book will be on the test. It is important to understand all major theories and concepts listed in the table of contents. It is also important to know any bolded words.

Don't worry if you do not understand or know a lot about the area. With minimal study, you can complete and pass the test.

Legal Note

All rights reserved. This Study Guide, Book and Flashcards are protected under the US Copyright Law. No part of this book or study guide or flashcards may be reproduced, distributed or stored in a retrieval system, or transmitted in any form or by any means, electronic, mechanical, photocopying, recording, or otherwise, without the prior written permission of the publisher Breely Crush Publishing LLC.

FLASHCARDS

This section contains flashcards for you to use to further your understanding of the material and test yourself on important concepts, names or dates. Read the term or question then flip the page over to check the answer on the back. Keep in mind that this information may not be covered in the text of the study guide. Take your time to study the flashcards, you will need to know and understand these concepts to pass the test.

| A-B-C model | ACA |

| Acculturation | Adlerian counseling |

| Affect-display actions | Affective domain |

| Americans with Disabilities Act (ADA) | Analytical perspective |

American Counseling Association. Primary representative association in the US. Focuses on validating and expanding counseling. 	Used in REBT. A= Situation, B=Belief, and C=Emotional response. 
Focuses on modifying client belief systems to create a healthier perspective. 	When a person adapts their own culture to accommodate elements of a new culture. 
Focused on non-cognitive understanding such as emotions, personality, interests, etc. 	Type of body language. Actions which convey emotions (i.e., expressions and gestures). 
Branch of psychodynamic theory which was developed by Carl Jung. Considers the collective unconscious. 	Requires that all public buildings are accessible to disabled individuals and prohibits discrimination. 

APA	Aptitude test
Assimilation	B. F. Skinner
Behavioral therapy	Body language
CACREP	Career development

Analytically based tests which are designed to assess the taker's abilities in a variety of different areas. 	American Psychological Association. Represents interests of and works to enhance the applications of psychology. 
Famed for developing the classical conditioning model of learning. 	The tendency for an original culture to be replaced by a new culture. 
Communication which relates to physical signals (i.e., posture, expression, eye movement, etc.). 	A type of therapy which focuses on helping clients improve their moods and attitudes through altering their actions. 
The process of career education, decision making, and guidance throughout an individual's life. 	Council for Accreditation of Counseling and Related Education Programs. 

Carl Rogers	Characteristics of good counselor
Civil Rights Act	Classical conditioning
Clinical psychology	Close-ended questions
Cognitive domain	Cognitive therapy

Good listener, leader, open personality, accepting, selfless, non-judgmental, selfconfident. 	Developed person-centered (client-centered) therapy model; a self-directive, humanistic therapy. 
Involves creating a link between a neutral stimulus and a desired response. First studied by Pavlov. 	Prohibits discrimination based on race, color, religion, gender, or nationality. 
Can be answered with a yes or no response. 	The treatment of a mentally ill individual, and the study of other behavioral anomalies and psychiatric problems. 
Asserts that clients can understand their own thought processes, that they have personal meanings, and that discovering the meanings will lead to improvement. 	Focused on intellectual, knowledge-oriented testing. 

Collective unconscious	**Consultation**
Counseling psychology	**Counter-transference**
Decisional career approaches	**Deinstitutionalization**
Dereflection	**Developmental career approaches**

A collaborative form of counseling in which counselors seek advice from each other. 	A collection of the universal human consciousness which extends from the beginning of the human race. 
When counselors shift emotions they have for other situations to their client relationships. 	Emphasis in treating otherwise healthy individuals who are struggling with problems of a psychological nature. 
A movement towards placing patients in localized community facilities offering outpatient care. 	Assume that people will maximize benefits and minimize losses. Expectancy theory and self-efficacy theory. 
Focus on career development as a process. Ginzberg and Super's theories. 	A distraction technique in logotherapy that attempts to draw attention away from the problem. 

| Dorothea Dix | DSM-IV |

| Dual relationship | Dynamic equilibrium |

| Eclectic therapy | Edmund Husserl |

| Edward Tichener | Emotional fusion |

The most accepted manual identifying and classifying mental and psychological issues.	Devoted her life to improving the treatment of mentally ill individuals (during mid-1800s).
A state in which things are constantly changing, and yet the overall balance of the system is maintained.	Occurs when counselor fills multiple roles with an individual.
Famed for developing phenomenological approach.	Characterized by a combination of multiple approaches in treatment of patients.
Occurs in families when no distinction or balance between emotions and feelings exists.	Worked with Wilhelm Wundt to develop structuralism.

Empathy	Erik Erikson
Ethnocentrism	Family counseling
Four consultation models	Four types of feminism
Frank Parsons	Freud's psychosexual stages

A psychoanalyst who documented stages of emotional growth in regards to human babies.	When one person sees that another person is suffering and they try to better understand them.
Involving entire families in the counseling process and treating them as a cohesive unit.	An individual's belief that their own culture is superior to all others.
Radical, liberal, cultural, social.	Mental health, training workshop, behavioral, and process.
Oral, anal, phallic, latency, and genital.	"The father of counseling" who sparked the vocational counseling movement.

Gestalt therapy	**Holistic therapy**
Humanistic therapy	**Incongruence (personcentered therapy)**
Jean Piaget	**Logotherapy**
Maslow's hierarchy of needs	**Mental health counseling**

Asserts that a person's mental, physical, and spiritual health are all connected.	Asserts that individuals attempting to change into something they are not causes stagnation. Attempts to help them reach a state of wholeness.
The difference in a perception of who they are vs. who they want to be.	Therapies based in the belief that individuals have the ability to seek personal growth and improve their lives.
Asserts that (a) all life has meaning, (b) people have a will to meaning, and (c) people can activate their will to meaning and pursue a better life.	Studied the development of children's understanding and developed a model of development.
Most directly involved in treating individuals with emotional conflicts and strains (anxiety, grief, stress).	Physical, safety, belonging and love, esteem, selfactualization.

Most consumed drug/ substance by teens	**Multicultural therapy**
Murray Bowen	**Naturalistic observation**
NBCC	**Nonverbal communication**
Open-ended questions	**Operant conditioning**

Considers the cultural factors relevant to a client's specific situation and struggles.	Alcohol.
Describes observing subjects in natural situations, without influencing them in any way.	Worked in field of family therapy. Developed concepts of differentiation and emotional fusion.
Important elements of effective communication which are not actually voiced.	National Board for Certified Counselors. Primary licensing board for counselors.
Involves creating an association between actions and consequences. Studied by Skinner.	Require more than simple yes or no response.

| Paradoxical intention | Paralanguage |

| Participant observation | Personality-based career approaches |

| Person-centered therapy | Preferred counseling for Hispanic clients |

| Psychodynamic therapy | Qualia |

Communication that occurs indirectly through verbal communication (i.e., through pitch, tone, etc.). 	An attempt to overemphasize a problem or phobia to eliminate a client's fear. Used in logotherapy. 
Assert that individuals are suited based on personality for certain careers. Roe's and Holland's theories. 	The observer/counselor is fully involved in the situation that they are observing. 
Family counseling. 	Also called client-centered. Strong emphasis on client-counselor relationship and eliminating incongruence.
An abstract term used in phenomenology to describe a person's unique perceptions. 	Attempts to identify and work through maladaptive functions of the subconscious. Asserts that actions are controlled by unconscious motivations. 

| Rational Emotive Behavior Theory (REBT) | Rehabilitation counseling |

| Reinforcement | Rorschach inkblot test |

| Satir's four dysfunctional communicators | Section 502 Rehabilitation Act |

| Section 504 Rehabilitation Act | Self-efficacy |

Specialize in work with individuals who are either disabled or recovering from serious injury.	Believes people naturally have good and bad behaviors. Emphasizes acceptance of self along with working towards good behaviors.
Bases interpretations about personality on an individual's response to a series of inkblots.	A pattern of punishment and rewards which can encourage or discourage behaviors.
Requires that federal buildings are transportationally accessible to disabled individuals.	Computer, Distractor, Placator, Blamer.
A person's perception of their ability to complete a task.	Requires that federal buildings are architecturally accessible to individuals with disabilities.

Shaping	Sigmund Freud
Simon-Binet scale	Social learning theory
Socratic dialogue	Somatic symptoms
Spirituality	Structuralism

Developed the psychoanalytic method and stages of psychosexual development.	Involves working toward gradual changes in behavior called successive approximations.
People can learn through observation, intrinsic factors also motivate learning, learning does not always change behavior.	Developed by Alfred Binet. First IQ test.
Physical symptoms. Often emphasized by cultures less trusting of counseling.	A technique in logotherapy involving active, questioning dialogue to help clients gain perspective.
Essentially the first major school of thought in psychology which attempted to deconstruct reactions to basic motives behind them.	Personal beliefs regarding intrinsic values and meanings in life.

Structured observation	Sympathy
Systematic desensitization	Systems therapy
Test reliability	Test validity
Trait and factor theory	Transference

A feeling of pity for a person who is suffering.	The observer defines ahead of time the elements and behaviors that they intent to observe.
Considers the interconnectedness of individuals in a population.	Process by which individuals train themselves to not be afraid through classical conditioning.
The extent to which a test actually tests the information it is meant to.	The extent to which a test is consistent among individuals.
When clients shift emotions they have for another person/ situation and applies them to counselor.	Involves classifying a person's individual characteristics (traits) to determine career aptitudes.

Triangulation	**Unfinished business**
Verbal communication	**Viktor Frankel**
Virginia Satir	**Vocational counseling**
When to break confidentiality	**Who a counselor's first responsibility is to**

Unresolved issues which have been pushed to the background. Important in Gestalt therapy. 	The creation of a triadic relationship involving the mother, father, and child. Created to relieve tension but creates vulnerability as well. 
Famed for developing logotherapy. 	Actually speaking with the client. Includes commenting, paraphrasing, discussion, etc. 
Focuses on helping individuals choose the most productive and satisfying career paths for themselves. 	Important to family therapy. Studied triadic relationships and dysfunctional communication patterns. 
Client/patient. 	When counselor's life is threatened, when the law requires it, when child abuse is involved, and when information is required in legal proceeding.